More Praise for *Writing Wild*

"*Writing Wild* brims with truths about living and writing and provides an invitation to live wild before we write. Tina Welling shatters conventional separations between mind and spirit, between the living and those who breathe but have forgotten how to live. She invites us back to nature and to remember what the species has forgotten."

— Gerry Spence, trial lawyer and author of
Seven Simple Steps to Personal Freedom

"Tina Welling teaches writers the most important lesson of all: how to pay attention. *Writing Wild* is a heartfelt book about learning the rules of creativity from nature and how to be alert through our five senses to this wild and beautiful world. This book is inspiring and valuable not only to writers but to all creative people."

— Barbara Abercrombie,
author of *A Year of Writing Dangerously*

"I know Tina Welling and have taught with Tina Welling, and I can think of no better person to trust a writer's education to than Tina. *Writing Wild* will be a welcome addition to any writer's library, a book that explores the natural world and its relation to the writing life."

— Craig Johnson, author of the Walt Longmire mysteries,
the basis of A&E's hit series *Longmire*

"Tina Welling shows us how openhearted attention to the natural world can take us beyond simple observation into a creative partnership with our surroundings. She takes us to a place where stories speak themselves and whisper reassuring truths, and then shows us how to use them in our own stories. Whatever you write, this book can make it better."

— Jeremy Schmidt, author of
Grand Canyon: The Life and Times of a Natural Treasure

"*Writing Wild* succeeds — on a spiritual as well as practical level — at connecting the head and the heart. By integrating these words, in all their simplicity and depth, an aspiring writer and lover of nature will arrive at a place well beyond their expectations."

— Broughton Coburn, author of
The Vast Unknown: America's First Ascent of Everest

"Before I was a full chapter into Tina Welling's book, I found myself breathing more deeply; by chapter 2, I was outside — with the book, my notebook, and a pen, smelling leaves of the lemon tree, examining a shiny snail trail on the sidewalk, and writing names for the color of the bougainvillea bracts on the back fence; by chapter 3, I'd made a list of people I wanted to give *Writing Wild* to. What a gentle guide and rich companion for explorations of our wilderness — both inside and out."

— Judy Reeves, author of *A Writer's Book of Days*

"These days we think *wild* equates with unruly violence, when really it means experiencing life from the right brain and body, via direct knowing and intuition — a skill so many of us have lost. Tina Welling connects you with a renewed wildness, a wide-eyed freshness that will gently focus your attention on the presence inside everything. This book will help you learn how to *really* see and come more fully alive. I love it!"

— Penney Peirce, author of
The Intuitive Way, *Frequency*, and *Leap of Perception*

"This book is as delightful as it is thoughtful. Spend a day with Tina Welling in the woods and feel your writer's heart burst open on the page. Tina has created a process in which you can learn — easily — to awaken and align your nature soul with your writer's soul, bringing greater richness and depth to both. This book will be a treasured companion of mine for a long, long time."

— Susan Chernak McElroy, author of *Animals as Teachers and Healers*

Writing Wild

Also by Tina Welling

Cowboys Never Cry

Crybaby Ranch

Fairy Tale Blues

Writing Wild

Forming a Creative Partnership with Nature

TINA WELLING

New World Library
Novato, California

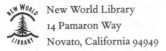

New World Library
14 Pamaron Way
Novato, California 94949

Excerpts from *Writing Wild* have been published in a different form in the following
magazines or syndicates: *Shambhala Sun*, *Writers on the Range*, *Teton Home and Living*, *Body & Soul*, *Natural Health*, *New Age*, and *The Writer*.

Text design by Tona Pearce Myers

Library of Congress Cataloging-in-Publication Data
Welling, Tina.
Writing wild : forming a creative partnership with nature / Tina Welling.
    pages   cm
Includes bibliographical references.
ISBN 978-1-60868-286-7 (pbk. : alk. paper) — ISBN 978-1-60868-287-4 (ebook)
  1. Authorship. 2. Creation (Literary, artistic, etc.) 3. Nature I. Title.
PN153.W43 2014
808.02—dc23   2013048987

First printing, May 2014
ISBN 978-1-60868-286-7
Printed in Canada on 100% postconsumer-waste recycled paper

New World Library is proud to be a Gold Certified Environmentally
Responsible Publisher. Publisher certification awarded by Green Press
Initiative. www.greenpressinitiative.org

10 9 8 7 6 5 4 3 2 1

To my sister,
Gayle Caston,
with love

Contents

Introduction

ONE SUMMER DAY, I hiked Josie's Ridge on Snow King Mountain. Large clouds moved across the sky and periodically put a lid over the sun. I paused to catch my breath from the upslope climb and gazed around the shadowy forest of tall, lanky pines. My glance caught on a fully rounded tree, leafless and apparently dead, standing upright with an abundance of sweeping limbs, making the tree stand out from others. At that moment, the sun broke through the cloud cover, and as I stood there, a dense, dew-beaded spiderweb, lacing the branches top to bottom, was abruptly illuminated.

One moment, the dead tree was notable only for its shapely flare, unusual in a harsh, high-altitude environment. The next moment, it was aflame with stars. My throat tightened, and tears stung my eyes. The forest was silent, I was alone, and the tree spangled before me, woven with fairy lights. Then the clouds closed over the sun again, and the sparkle was gone.

I stood in those shadowy woods looking at the bare tree, and my mind experienced a gracious leap. Skipping over the small steps of understanding, I knew suddenly that there was an interconnectedness between the earth's creative energy and my own personal creative energy.

Writing Wild was conceived right then. I wanted to understand more about this connectedness. I wanted to explore those small intuitive steps of knowing — to lay them out one by one, untangle the workings of that connection, and learn how to use this natural resource.

In our daily lives, you and I may be unaware that everything we know about creating, we know intuitively from the natural world. Yet when the light shines just right, we sense that we are part of the whole energy system of the universe, poised endlessly to express itself.

Writing Wild is based on the ancient universal law "As above, so below," which tells us we can understand the patterns of the higher by following the patterns of the lower, and vice versa. In the case of writing, by following the patterns of the earth's creative energy, we can understand our own personal creative energy. Though the interconnectedness of ourselves and the natural world shimmers like the spider's web in sunlight, at times it can be so subtle that, not seeing it at all, we walk right into it, the supple strands clinging to our face and fingers. When the light shines directly on the web of connectedness, I think to myself, "Why write this book? Everybody sees this web sparkling like an earthbound constellation." But other times, when the web disappears before my eyes, I realize that as a creative person, I am often floundering, feeling a lack of support and guidance, unaware I am entangled in my own safety net.

Joseph Campbell once said, "The goal of life is to make your heartbeat match the beat of the universe, to match your nature with Nature." Capital *N*. Following his advice, I developed a simple *three-step process*: naming, describing, and interacting. These three steps address the levels of our awareness and correlate with the three parts of our brain. I call the process a Spirit Walk to remind me of the spirit of my experience.

Writing Wild offers writers, journal keepers, and those others of us who wish to live more fully a direct pathway into *a stronger relationship with wildness*, both inner and outer. The result is writing that inspires, heals, enlivens, and deeply engages both writer and reader.

Writing constellates what we feel and intuit in our bodies and know in our psyches. Once we *name, describe,* and *interact* with our experience in writing, the experience belongs to us consciously and contributes to our creative work.

Spiderwebs are both wondrous and ordinary. The silk created to weave a web is a protein the spider produces from eating houseflies and other insects. Nothing more ordinary than houseflies. Yet nothing is more wondrous than the spangled web. The topics discussed in *Writing Wild* are ordinary as well, and consist of practical, down-to-earth ideas and experiences. But they serve to ensure that when the sun tips just a fraction of one degree and lights up the whole world before us, we are present to enjoy it.

CHAPTER ONE

Spirit Walks

I ONCE READ AN ACCOUNT OF A WOMAN who had been struck by lightning, causing her severe nerve damage. Afterward, what mattered in her life changed completely, and she felt grateful for the experience. Except for the nerve damage, this was what happened to me when I began to wake up to the world around me.

It all started with a postcard.

I was on my way to opening the Rosebud, my resort shop in Jackson Hole, Wyoming, but stopped first at the health-food store to pick up coffee and pastry. There it was, right on the counter, a postcard with a picture of earth taken from space. Against a shiny black sky, our planet glowed with swirly blues and purples, framed by two lines of a message: "Wake up! You live here!"

Normally, my first concern might have been the overuse of exclamation points, but this morning the message itself punched me smack in the chest and set off an alarm inside. I had just been outdoors, but I couldn't say what the sky looked like, cloudy or clear, or whether birds sang or if I'd felt a breeze on my cheeks.

I had been locked inside my head, thinking. I didn't live with awareness inside my own body, much less on the earth.

After that, a phrase I'd heard all of my life, "Come to your senses," began to take on new meaning. I abruptly awakened to my senses, to dramatic consequence. My husband joked about an alien spirit descending into my body. But it was just me. I descended into my body.

Yet things don't really happen all of a sudden, I know. They just seem to occur that way. It certainly seemed to my husband, John, and even to me that I'd changed suddenly. But I believe now that the changes just took time to accumulate. It's like the arrival of spring; it happens so gradually that we think it sudden — the moment we notice the tatting of green on bare tree limbs.

Looking back, I realize that getting in touch with my creative energy began the process of alerting me to life. I changed bit by bit, over many years, as I dove deeper into my writing and my relationship with the natural world. I liked this heightened awareness, and I wanted to be even more conscious of life around me. That morning in the health-food store, I was tapped on the shoulder by life itself, and I was finally ready to answer the call.

I began to spend more time outdoors, taking my black-and-white shaggy pup, Tess, for leisurely three- and four-mile hikes along Flat Creek. Yet, often, I was still sleepwalking, unaware of my surroundings and deep in my thoughts. I could miss the most wonderful things along the path: sunlight through golden aspen leaves, the sound of creek water clattering the rocks. I would come home exercised, but not enlivened.

I wanted to be wake-walking.

I began to break down how perception moved through

consciousness. I wanted to learn how to cooperate with my natural system to get fully awake on my planet. When I figured it out, I categorized the information into a three-step process that correlated to the work of the three parts of the brain: reptile, midbrain, and neocortex. I called my outings Spirit Walks, to remind me to be aware of the spirit of my experience. Throughout this research, layers and layers of understanding unfolded, and once I began to use that knowledge, a whole new world of awareness opened to me. Many unexpected gifts surfaced, and those ideas are discussed in the following chapters.

The three-step process discussed here was inspired by a book I was reading at the time, called *The Intuitive Way*. In it, author Penney Peirce describes how information travels through our bodies and minds, alerting our conscious awareness. In general, the first level of awareness in our bodies arises from *instinct* — desire, pain, pleasure. Our senses trigger awareness of these primitive urges the way touching a baby's cheek induces the baby to make sucking motions or the way saliva is released before we know consciously that we smell apple pie.

The information then moves into the conscious awareness of our senses: we know we smell apple pie and begin to look for the aroma's source. Next *emotion* arises in response to what our senses bring us — perhaps we experience a fleeting desire to be cared for or comforted. Then we create meanings and associations between sensory information and our inner life: hopes, memories, fears, and dreams. We remember Grandma and her apple pie; we wonder whether we'll ever taste one again. Finally, the data moves into the *language* area of the brain, where we can label and sort it into abstract ideas and definite plans. If we call

Grandma and tell her we've been dreaming about her apple pie, maybe she'll give us the recipe.

This mental pathway corresponds with the three-part formula for a Spirit Walk: *naming*, which serves to alert our conscious awareness to the senses; *describing*, which engages our senses and body responses on a deeper, more intimate level; and *interacting*, which invites us to create a relationship with our surroundings.

Our five senses are our doorways into a fuller experience of our bodies, our writing, and our planet. When I consciously take in the fragrance of pine, the acknowledgment attaches my feet to the ground I stand on, the space I share with the pine tree. I reside more fully in my muscles, my bones, and I become aware of how the emotions aroused by my senses act on my organs and their systems. And then I want to tell someone about it.

Pen and paper are the only tools needed for a Spirit Walk. When we write, we pull the whole of ourselves — body, mind, and soul — into engaging with the unconscious and bringing ourselves into full awareness.

Here's how a recent Spirit Walk worked for me:

With a notebook and pen, I headed out to hike on the top of Snow King Mountain on a blue-sky morning in early June, just before the crowds of summer tourists arrive here in Jackson Hole. This decision meant a ride on the chairlift, which in the past I'd used only during ski season. I've always enjoyed the ride then because you can see a hundred miles away into Yellowstone and feel eye to eye with the peaks of the Grand Tetons.

But on this morning, the ride up the mountain frightened me. I was puzzled; the lift had never bothered me before. Now my chest felt constricted; I longed to pull in a deep, satisfying breath but couldn't. My toes ached from gripping the insoles of my hiking boots, and my hands were sweaty on the safety bar. In the winter, the resort removed these safety bars so skiers could slip on and off the chairs quickly, so why was I scared with one today? Shouldn't I feel more secure with it locked in place before me? It helped if I didn't move, not even my eyes. So much for the beautiful view I was looking forward to seeing. I stared straight ahead, tried not to blink, and hung on tightly.

Once I reached the summit of Snow King, I stepped gratefully off the chairlift onto solid ground and took a deep breath. Remembering the postcard that served as a tap on the neurons — "Wake up! You live here!" — I started to *name* things I saw. Large things came to my attention first: mountain peaks, clouds, boulders. I wrote them down in my notebook. Then I used my other senses and began to notice smaller things: the cry of a redtail hawk, the powdery feel of aspen bark, the fragrance of damp earth. Awareness followed a certain order as the senses descended into my less conscious areas, from sight to sound, touch, taste, and smell.

The point was to make a quick list, so I moved on.

As I walked, I kept my senses attuned to my surroundings and gathered more information. Tearing off a leaf of sagebrush, I crushed it in my palm and inhaled the fresh, herby scent; I chewed another leaf and quickly spit it out. Not the same sage we stuff into a turkey.

Across a narrow ridge, with the Tetons flaring snowy peaks on one side and the Gros Ventre Mountains rolling into eternity on the other, I walked up a rocky outcropping and found a place to sit beneath a twisted pine. Out with the notebook and pen again for the second part of my Spirit Walk: *describing*, or *detailing*.

I looked for something that especially attracted me and chose a pinecone. As if I were making an intricate drawing, I used language to describe the feel of the pinecone against my cheek, rippled a thumbnail down its scales near my ear — this could be a new musical instrument — and touched my tongue to its dry woodiness. "It tastes better than the sagebrush leaf," I wrote in my notebook, "but I'd rather have a Snickers bar." Still, we love what we know, and I had offered this pinecone my full attention. We had a relationship.

I rose and hiked deeper into the forest, listening to the silence, which filled with its own details as soon as I named them: insect buzz, wind rustling my hair, pine needles crunching underfoot, my own breath. I walked around a tall, leafless bush and was abruptly arrested by the way its fuzzy catkins, backlit by the sun, glistened silver against the blue sky. I felt the surprise and joy of Christmas morning. I recalled plugging in the Christmas tree my husband and I decorated when first married. We were so poor that we formed chicken wire into a cone around a pole and stuff it with green florist paper. No ornaments, only lights.

With this memory, I slipped into the third part of my Spirit Walk. I had opened myself to place and allowed an exchange, or *interaction*, between the outer world of nature and my inner world of emotion and intimate experience.

I hiked deeper into the woods and looked for a place where I could write about the catkins glowing like Christmas bulbs. Up ahead, a lodgepole pine had grown with a crook in its trunk. Probably when it was young, this tree had formed around a dead tree that had fallen across it. The deadfall had long ago decayed, but the crook it created made a perfect seat for me. I hoisted myself up and got comfortable as if I were sitting in the tree's lap. I began to swing my legs.

Like a smoothly spliced movie tape, the image of a Ferris wheel surfaced. My father and I sat together at the top of the Ferris wheel as it stopped to load new riders, and he began to swing his legs. I was young, about nine years old, and this scared me. My father laughed and teased me by pumping harder. The seat swayed, and I clenched the safety bar, rigid with alarm. I imagined the seat looping right over the top from my father's movements and me falling out, screaming past all the lights strung on the big wheel. Either my father didn't believe my fear was real, or he believed he could tease me past it. But my fear was real, and I never moved past it. I never went on a Ferris wheel again, with or without my father.

I was writing all this down, my notebook resting on my knees, my shoulder leaning against the rough bark of the lap tree.

Suddenly, I got it. The chairlift. The reason it scared me today during the summer, when it never had during the winter. The memory hit the light of consciousness, and I felt the beginnings of release from my fear. Now that I understood it, I knew I could stir up the courage to climb back on the chairlift for my return trip down the mountain.

At this point, I had been outside only an hour, but my experience had been one of fullness both inwardly and outwardly. I had become aware of a fear that had been hidden from my consciousness for decades, and I also carried a deeper relationship with this mountaintop, its pinecones and new spring growth, its bird cries and sage aromas. I had looked closely at the dirt beneath my feet and learned it consisted of insect parts, pine needles, stone chips, wildflower seeds. It was made up of pieces of its surroundings, just as I was made up of pieces of my surroundings.

My Spirit Walk was complete.

CHAPTER TWO

Do It Yourself

ONCE I KNEW HOW TO FULLY INHABIT MY WORLD through using the senses, I wanted never to lose my way again. Though at times I still find myself locked inside my head with thoughts, I know how to reenter my body now and return to wake-walking. I have given new meaning to the acronym *BYOB*. Instead of the party message "bring your own bottle," to me it means "bring your own body." And every time I do, I find myself waking up to enjoy a fuller experience of living on this swirly blue-and-purple planet of ours.

Naming, Detailing, Interacting

As stated earlier, the three steps of a Spirit Walk follow the pathway by which our brains absorb and release back out our life's experiences. The process also mimics the pattern of life as a whole. We begin our relationship with the world during childhood by *naming* — singling out parents and food, labeling them, giving our bodies the job of learning to pronounce the sounds that match the people and things. Next we notice *details* and sort these into *descriptions* — this blue, fuzzy blanket, not that yellow, smooth one. We distinguish our experiences by what we notice with our senses. Then we *interact*. We create relationships with those parents and others we have named; we bond with teddy bears and crackers.

A two-year-old girl came into my shop one day, and while her mother looked through ski hats, the little girl headed toward a basket of toy flowers on the floor. "Flower," she whispered to herself, then held one of them up to her nose. She had learned to name this item, to describe it, and to interact with what she had named "flower," through her senses. A flower was supposed to have fragrance. These plush flowers with bendable stems did not have fragrance, and the little girl could not believe her nose. She went through a dozen of them, squatting on the floor, smelling each one, her face intent on the mystery. It was, in its own way, heartbreaking; I wanted so much for her to be confirmed in what she was learning about the world. We as adults are still going through this process of naming, describing, and interacting. It would be most desirable to go through the process consciously, I thought, as this little girl was doing.

Whatever we can bring into the light of consciousness, we can use in our life's work. Whatever stays hidden in the dark of our unconscious is using us.

Before realizing the story behind my fear of swinging seats with safety bars, I was paralyzed, in the grip of this fear, unable to combat it with anything other than the willpower not to wail loudly until someone lowered me to the ground. Willpower is not a useful tool in the long run when it comes to our inner lives. It's just a Band-Aid for the moment. For the long run, we want to bring up the hidden stories, present them to the light, and let them guide us toward living more fully.

In my case, I needed to honor the feelings of this experience, comfort the nine-year-old self that lived through it, and address the choices it presented to my adult self. I learned many things from that Ferris wheel story. From my body, I learned that often I will deal with unpleasant situations by holding on tight and pushing through them. My impetus on the chairlift to not move any part of my body, including my eyes, matches my desire not to rock the boat or even look around for alternatives in a situation in which I am uncomfortable, even miserable. I don't easily change my position or impose my feelings on others. It's not easy for me to stand up for myself. For someone else, a similar experience may reveal the depths of fear he feels near his father, or anxiety over being out of control, or perhaps a fear of heights. Each of us will unearth our own personal stories and reach insights particular to our unconscious selves.

Later, I'll discuss how we can use the stories we unearth during a Spirit Walk for our creative projects as well as our self-awareness. Simple writing exercises can contact wisdom from within ourselves to match any call for healing, once we become conscious of the need. In every case, our healing lies side by side with our wounds. Our answers come from the exact place our questions arise. Where else would they be?

Those of us who are creative writers use our senses, all five, as the palette from which we draw connectedness between ourselves and our readers. Our bodies are the tools of our trade. We tell our personal stories through the communal language of our physical selves and our planet.

Do It Yourself

Here's how to take yourself on a Spirit Walk:

Any season, any weather, dress comfortably, go outside. Head for your backyard, a school playground, a city park, the wilderness. At some point, do more than walk on the earth. Sit down, lie down (even if you need to brush a couple feet of snow off a fallen tree, as I often do), set your butt right on nature itself. In my case, if I sit too long during the colder parts of the Wyoming winter, my behind freezes to the layer of snow I'm sitting on — this is my way of suggesting I'm not open to excuses here. Get outside; it's an important piece of the process. Pull out your notebook and pen, and make a list of what you see, hear, touch, taste, smell. One-word lists work well. Sight is the easiest sense for most of us. We spend a lot of time in our heads and use terms of sight to mean understanding or other ways of knowing: *I see, I've lost sight of it, I'm eyeing it*. The goal here is to widen our experience beyond the mental perception. The ear, in fact, has three times more connections to the brain than the eye does. So let's move into listing sounds.

We are descending from the more conscious senses to those nearer instinct. Sight is the farthest from instinct; smell is closest. We move down into our bodies as we open to the natural world around us. The act of writing weaves our inner and outer environments together. It makes us conscious of our bodies and of the earth and brings the whole experience into physical form — words on paper. Naming pins down experience so that we can feel it all the way through ourselves and communicate it to others. Anyone who has been sick and not had a name for the condition from which they were suffering understands the ease that arrives along with the diagnosis. Despite the bad news the label may bring, there is comfort in the naming and a way now to communicate about the condition with others and a pathway toward dealing with it.

For step 2 of your Spirit Walk, get up and walk for a ways in the outdoors. Stop when you feel like it. Choose one thing: a stone, a twig, a leaf, something you can handle and touch. Think twice about choosing a bug; the next step is to describe this one thing using your senses — for some of us, bugs are not that appealing to taste. Sit down and write, in paragraph form or as a list, all the details you can about your chosen item.

Notice your body responses and write those as well. Are you comfortable? Taking deep breaths or shallow ones? Stomach relaxed or knotted? Muscle aches? No judgments about any of this, just reports from your body. It may be the first time some of us have given this much attention to our physical selves. Tell it all — let your body speak up — but don't be surprised if not all that much information arises just yet. Many of us have numbed out our body sensations for so long we need a few opportunities for communication channels to reopen.

That was true for me. Somewhere along the line, I had taught myself to respond to pain by willing my attention elsewhere. I got so good at this that I could walk into a sharp-edged coffee table, whack my shin on it, move away without acknowledging the pain, and wonder later during my bath what the heck the purple swelling was about.

For step 3 of your Spirit Walk, get up and move again to another part of the outdoors. Walk with awareness of your senses, your body, of the wildness around you and the emotions you experience in it. Feel the earth beneath your feet supporting you; tip your face into the wind; describe a cloud to yourself;

warm the palms of your hands in sunlight; notice how your hips move with each step, how your arms swing; smell the air and listen for birdsong; identify flavors in your mouth — perhaps left over from lunch, from toothpaste, or from that bug I warned you about tasting.

Walk until you realize you are recalling a memory, or feeling emotions, or having thoughts connected to a past event. These are your stories. Do not dismiss a single one — we tend to do that; we've been dismissing ourselves in big and small ways much of our lives. Write the stories down. Analyze them, if you'd like, but later. Now is the time for becoming conscious of the stories and for capturing them in words.

Name, *describe*, *interact*. These three things can be done in a total of five minutes during break time at work or enjoyed during a daylong outing.

A Deeper Experience of Life

So how does a Spirit Walk improve our writing skills?

Life is a good news / bad news situation. The bad news is that we are all going to die someday. The good news is that we get to live until we do. As writers, we need to live more fully than others; most certainly, writers need to live more fully than their readers. We must be exquisitely aware of ourselves and our surroundings and the life force that throbs within us continuously.

Some writers in the past have thought that living fully meant drinking heavily, experiencing many adventures, having a variety of lovers, and putting themselves in life-threatening danger. A full life, as many viewed it, was found at the extremes. I think of Ernest Hemingway running with the bulls, fighting in a war, deep-sea fishing, hunting big game, and then returning home to use the material as background for his writing. These activities looked glamorous to readers who were struggling through war or the depression that followed. Bland lifestyles and limited choices described the daily lives of most people during those times. Now the lives of most readers are busy; they are overscheduled and multitasking during the week and enjoying a variety of adventures on the weekends. Even shopping is an adventure compared to what it was decades ago. Almost everyone can experience drinking a lot and having a variety of lovers, and life-threatening danger is as close as the nearest expressway.

Readers still desire reading about experiences that are not easily accessible to them, but that desire has changed from a *broader* experience of life to a *deeper* experience of life, one with intensity and fullness and intimacy uncommon to most of us. Just as we require our visual artists to offer us new and varied perspectives of the world, a writer is required to offer readers more-concentrated perspectives of the world — views of life that are exquisitely depicted, original, and authentic. A writer can't fake that. A writer must have experienced the wild edges of aliveness in order to write about them with vivid truth.

Creative writers can no longer be just observers. There are scientists for that. We can't just be recorders of scene and activity; there are historians for that. The new tradition demands that writers hold some of all that *and also create a brand-new event out of it with our experience and our use of language.* This is the process of a Spirit Walk. This is writing wild.

We make our work throb. We don't just see stars overhead or the configurations they create — the Big Dipper, Orion's Belt — or merely know the myths and legends behind them, but all that and more. We must have a relationship with those stars. Know them in our body, feel them burn our skin, sense their light pinning us to the planet. Allow them to stir our personal stories.

Tens of thousands of people visit my hometown from all over the world. The beauty in Jackson Hole is overwhelming to many. The Tetons soar straight up from wildflower meadows into rocky peaks; nearby Yellowstone steams, geysers spurt against the blue sky, and hot pots bubble inside pastel formations. Bison, elk, and moose graze in view on the drive from the airport. People fly in here for vacation and between the airport and the town square, they become glazed over with stimulation they can't process. They tend to pull out cameras in order to savor it later, when they return home, like television.

Yet we can't postpone the process of connecting to a sense of place. That is an experience of the present moment only and involves our full sensory ability, our body, emotions, and mind. We miss the experience when we hide behind a camera, and later we have the evidence of only one of the five senses — sight.

Still, many of us behave like tourists in our own lives. If we can't put a frame around our experience, we may choose to numb out from the present moment altogether, and so we need to mark our experiences in order to be conscious of them. Our job, for ourselves and for our readers, is to mark them fully, deeply, intimately. The organization of the three-step process of a Spirit Walk helps us do that.

Asked in an interview for the book *The Dream of the Marsh Wren* how she would write a poem if transported to another planet, the poet Pattiann Rogers replied, "I would start with the senses, and I would describe a physical object very carefully and then see if anything else rose out of that." She says, "In the particular object lies all that I discover."

A Spirit Walk is a writer's form of meditation. We still ourselves, take in life around us through our senses, pulling it deep within our bodies and letting it stir responses from our emotions and minds. As writers, we capture our amplified awareness on paper, and our stories and language take on a vibrancy and authenticity that only come from true experience.

CHAPTER THREE

Writing into Truth

ONE DAY, I went into a bookstore and asked if they had any books on writing. Sometimes when my energy gets stuck, I like to read about the art of writing or about other writers. It helps. This day the saleswoman said, "We did have a section on writing, but a woman came in and said she was going to write a novel and took the whole shelf of books."

I didn't say so then, but I knew it: that woman was not going to write a novel or anything else. She was going to read.

Inner Authority

Like the woman in the bookstore, we are often seeking a source of authority. We think it's *out there* somewhere, when all along it's within us. Even when we do discover our inner authority, we often judge it by outer standards — and usually find it lacking. We can accrue dozens of excellent reviews with our latest book and believe it was a fluke or that we just fooled everybody. On the same day a friend learned his novel was on the *New York*

Times bestseller list, he also read an email from one disgruntled reader, and it ruined his day.

Many of us carry a kind of superstition about our inner power or creative energy. Even well-known, successful writers attribute their creative flow to how their desk or their day is arranged. Some writers need special pens or colored paper; others need to eat particular food or wear specific clothing when beginning the day's work. The poet Dame Edith Sitwell needed to lie in a coffin before starting her work. This behavior is a kind of religion based on outer signs that have worked for a writer once before. If a writer succeeded in having an especially vivid creative experience while wearing a plaid flannel bathrobe, he may wish to repeat the outfit the next day of writing.

Because we don't understand creative energy — where it comes from, how it rises into consciousness, how it's accessed or restored — we gather myths around it. We talk of it as *other*, as a muse that visits or an idea that strikes as haphazardly as lightning, an accident that just occurs. When work isn't going well, my sister, Gayle, finds herself thinking back to when work did go well. She recalls events that preceded that experience and considers anything she can do to reverse the negative tone of the moment. She laughs and says, "Some days I totally understand virgin sacrifices."

If this ancient ritual worked, we'd still do it. We'd sacrifice a first-time published novelist. Dress him up in ink-stained robes, have a parade, ask him to bless our pencils. And who knows? Maybe we'd feel better. For a while.

I know a man who teaches in the English department of a West Coast university throughout the school year and, for the past twenty-two years, has worked as a ranger in Grand Teton

National Park in the summers. He is so knowledgeable and enthusiastic about the park that he has been the ranger assigned to guide visiting presidents. Lee also writes; several of his books have been published.

One summer day, we had lunch together to catch up on the nine months since we'd last met. But first he told me what happened that morning on his way to work. As Lee tells it, he was driving to his check-in point in the park and was stuck for miles behind a park utility truck going ten miles under the speed limit. Lee became agitated, and his frustration turned into anger, which mounted to rage — a typical pattern, he confessed to me. So he laid on his horn, and when the utility truck didn't respond, Lee drove into the oncoming lane beside the truck, leaned over toward the passenger-side window, and yelled insults at the driver. He then swerved dangerously around the truck on a curve, almost meeting an oncoming car, and crowded the utility truck right off the road. Lee gave the truck driver the finger and sped away.

The trouble was that Lee was driving a park vehicle with official ranger ID plastered all over it.

"So," he told me, "I know I'm a jerk, now the truck driver knows I'm a jerk, and he's going to report me for being one to my supervisor." Lee wiped a palm down his face, rested his chin on his chest, and looked at me sheepishly, like a ten-year-old who's pulled a cute trick on his teacher. "The thing is," he said, "I think if I fix this anger deal, it'll mess up my writing." He paused, watched himself turn his glass of iced tea in a circle, then lifted his eyes. "Know what I mean?"

I did. I knew what he meant. From past conversations, I understood that Lee felt in awe of his rage as well as his creative source. Both were examples of Lee experiencing his power. Rage may be an immature expression of power, a primitive form of power, but it is power nonetheless; and often, we need the impressiveness of the emotion to fire up our inner authority. For example, nice people can go along with considerable abuse, but finally they are enabled by their anger to shout, "No!" That's good, but the idea is to get cues from *rising* feelings that something is happening emotionally that's important to us. And then to honor the emotion early with appropriate action.

Lee was a person who honored the emotion — anger — and stopped there. He felt a reverence for it. He didn't want to look too closely at his anger, and neither did he want to look too closely at the source of his creative energy. In his mind, his rage was coming from the same place as his enthusiasm when his writing flowed well or he was excitedly explaining the geological formations to a group of hikers.

I've heard Lee lecture on the trail; he sounds as mesmerizing as the wind. His animated features beneath his park-ranger hat, as he stands on the ledge at Inspiration Point, with the open sky as background, express his passion for the wilderness. His words soar out of him as his arm sweeps toward the mountain range across the lake. He's a Shakespearean actor, he's riveting, he's powerful. He's Lee. And he thinks that if he looks too deeply into what makes up this powerhouse called Lee, he might dismantle not just his quick and raging anger, but also his charisma as a lecturer in the classroom and on the trail, and as a writer on the page.

It's understandable that he feels this way; a lot of us do. Yet the truth is that we can shine the light into all our sources of power without fear of loss. In fact, it's our job to do so.

Spelunking Our Inner Selves

Traveling our unmapped inner caves, headlamps clamped on, is not scary; knowing we can get to this place of deep, honest, original power at will is exciting. We own all that we need within. Our minds, bodies, and emotions provide endless reference material — an inner library, really. And it is accessed through our senses. Unlike the lady who bought the shelf of writing books in preparation for beginning a novel, we can take charge of our own authority. We don't have to buy anything, attend special schools, wear particular clothes, travel anywhere. Best of all, we don't have to lie in a coffin like Dame Edith Sitwell before we write. Though at least there would be a plan to follow — drink coffee, shower, lie in coffin, write. The truth is that we are not dependent upon these things.

My friend Geneen lights a candle before writing, to remind herself to reach deeply for her very best. Kirsten begins her writing session with yoga. She says, "It makes my body happier about sitting still for a long period of time." Susan has a favorite rock from the top of Steamboat Mountain, the location of the novel she's working on, and a piece of deer antler that she likes to handle as she settles into her work place. Each woman knows that her skill does not depend on the ritual, but rather the ritual invites her creative energy to become engaged and focused.

Few of us are born knowing how to write, so along with discovering our inner truth, we need the necessary creative skills to carry out our work. The good news is that these, too, reside within each of us. We only need reminders once in a while about how to tap into this source and practice using these skills to their best advantage.

The ABCs of Writing into Truth

The ABCs of writing into our own truth are *attention, belief,* and *courage. Attention* means offering awareness to our body sensations and our emotions; *belief* means trusting our responses; *courage* means taking action based upon our responses. Each time we follow these ABCs, we strengthen the access to our inner authority. When we write down the discoveries our attention brings us — our emotions and body awareness — and read this back to ourselves or someone else, we are taking a step toward trusting our findings and taking action on them.

We don't have to know something to write; we write to know something. We write to bring into our consciousness the inner authority that so often remains in the unconscious. If you doubt at all your inner well of knowledge and creativity, stop right here and write a paragraph about any object in your vicinity. Report the findings of your senses and your body sensations. Allow associations to occur and images to arise.

People often ask writers, "Where do you get your ideas, your stories?" Even we wonder sometimes where our material comes from, especially when we are writing in a concentrated way that flows with newly unearthed material. Some writers give over their power and their reverence to the product — the book or poem — rather than the source of that product: their own inner authority. That's another result of thinking that the source is one of luck, of mystery, and feeling superstitious about examining that too closely, fearing it will disappear. Possibly, this accounts for those writers who have enormous success with one book and then can't write another. They've put all their power into the outcome of what is an inner process. Sadly, this sometimes happens with a person's first poem or story. It receives rave responses, and the writer believes it was a fluke because she can't trace the flow of the work from within her to the product without. She believes it was a onetime accident and, after the immediate exhilaration of her experience, becomes depressed. Oddly, this can happen even after multiple successes. One of my workshop students reports that he sees each publication as a fluke and fears he can't ever do it again.

It's this inner process of arriving at our own material that intrigues me and that I intend to demystify in this book. For if we don't understand it, we feel that creative energy is in control and shares itself with us only on whim. Our relationship to writing and to ourselves must be more intimate than that. Intimacy, in partnership with another human or in partnership with our inner selves, demands trust and faithfulness. We can't write if we think a disembodied muse may or may not show up to unlock our creative vault and give us access to our own personal material. This kind of thinking is irresponsible, as if we are refusing to be accountable for our own creative lives.

Material can occur to us, when we're open to it, with such rapidity that we cannot immediately trace the steps our minds took in connecting two seemingly unrelated ideas. But when we are very alert to the data our senses bring us and to the memories, hopes, fears, and dreams that the sensory data trigger, we will make instantaneous links. It's this fully traceable process that many of us mistake for mystery, luck, and visits from the muse. We often call it intuition.

Intuition is usually referred to as the sixth sense, as if it were an invisible sense organ of its own. Yet it may be that intuition is the exquisite use of the five senses we already know so well. Every event, every object, every feeling and thought has a network of veins connecting it to other events and objects, feelings, and thoughts.

To write is to become conscious of that interconnectedness.

A surgeon may have every reason to believe, along with his medical team, that it's time to close up a patient, job complete. Yet he hesitates and says, "Just a minute here." He doesn't know why he triple-checks his work right then; maybe it isn't until he finds a place in need of further attention that he realizes he was reacting to a whiff of odor. Maybe he never realizes why he hesitated; maybe the surgeon, along with his staff, chooses to believe that he has special powers or that he's lucky or that a guardian angel watches over him.

Yet possibly, the surgeon was acutely alert, fully present in his body, place, and time, allowing an instantaneous flow of information to rise from his body into his mind and emotions. He followed the ABCs of life. He offered his attention, he believed the information he received, and he had the courage to act on it, despite a roomful of people who thought differently. Living from our intuition or inner authority doesn't involve only the body; understanding and caring are at work as well. The surgeon needed to understand what to do with his information, and he needed to care that his work was being accomplished to his fullest ability.

At this moment, your presence in the place you are reading these words connects you to all that surrounds you. If you are outdoors, your exhaled breath is being inhaled by trees, flowers, weeds, and grasses. The ground is imprinted by your body. What a loss if we are not also conscious of how the energy of nature's presence affects us. Our goal is to work toward making our lives an exchange with the world around us.

CHAPTER FOUR

Engage Curiosity

INSTEAD OF FOLLOWING THE OLD RULE about writing about what we know, I propose writing about what we *want* to know. That draws us into following our curiosity. Curiosity is a powerful motivator.

We hold a valuable tool in the simple form of questions. Questions open new space. I think of a question the way the punctuation mark actually looks: like a hook, a hook used to grab further information.

The act of asking questions and writing until answers come works for me whether I am trying to sort out a friendship problem or figure out the plot of a short story. And yet answers themselves are not our highest goal. What we really want is feedback to our question, an enhanced field of awareness in which to examine our concern. So while we hold our question, we are stirring up an awareness of our body sensations, emotional responses, and often more questions.

More important than the immediate gratification of getting answers to things that puzzle us is feeling comfortable with not knowing, because that's just life. In a recent issue, the Buddhist magazine *Tricycle* ran a cartoon that says, "Don't worry that you don't understand stuff. It will probably stay that way."

At first, that cartoon annoyed me. I thought, "How can they say that? It's not funny, if that's what they think." Then I let the message sink in a moment and found the idea made my body relax. Right, I don't know, and I probably won't know. And that's okay.

Asking *why* or *how* is our way of drilling a shaft into the darkness in order to cast light upon the unknown. Questions come from the chaos inside us, all that uncertainty with which we live. Confusion is so prevalent in our lives that it could be called a universal state of mind. Yet, if we can form a question from that confusion, it helps organize our thoughts and emotions and give us focus.

I've found that the best way to ask our question is to engage our curiosity and let go of grasping for an answer, remembering that we are not trying to solve anything, but rather inviting clarity on the subject. The value of asking a question is that it requires us to organize our thoughts in order to form the question. And it's the vacuum created by the question that draws the responses.

Questions work as magnets, pulling in the information we desire.

A question arises from chaos, a field of disorganized uncertainty. The magnet that draws our attention to the chaotic field may be curiosity in positive situations: This is nice. How can I get more? Or in negative situations, the magnet may be concern: This is a problem. How can I fix it? The desire for satisfaction creates the need to form the question.

The question emerges; we clarify it and cast it back into the field of chaos, allowing responses to attach. Questions and responses are paired together; if you grab one, the other will follow.

Three steps: first, consider a concern that you presently carry; second, form it into a clear question; third, hold open a space for the response.

We are not always directed by a process during our writing into truth. We may be in so much pain and confusion that all we can do is write, and keep on writing until we feel the knotted ball of misery unraveling a bit more with each word. Eventually, we will stumble upon an insight and an action we can take. The satisfaction of experiencing our ability to name our feelings and thoughts, and describe them until we discover a response we can enact, strengthens our inner authority and ensures our future access to it.

When I follow an inner/outer rhythm of attention, I discover the proper question and responses to it without as much anxiety as when I concentrate only on my inner experience. Our surroundings can ease our stress and often carry clues to our inner world. And if I am outdoors, then I am supported and soothed by the enlivening energy around me.

First, I report in writing whatever I am conscious of at the moment. That may be as vague as a sense of uneasiness with my manuscript or that I feel puzzled about why I don't want to be around a certain coworker. A question is formed: Why do I feel this way? I describe my discomfort: how it makes my body feel, what emotions I am aware of, thoughts that arise. Then I report what is happening around me, checking in with my five senses. Perhaps I spot a white butterfly, hear water dripping, or smell pine sap. I write that down along with any associations that occur to me. Again I spiral through the three places in my consciousness: body, emotions, thoughts. And again I draw into the process the awareness of what is occurring around me in the natural world — insect buzz, humidity in the air, the flat light of a cloudy sky.

The idea is to bring up emotions, associations, memories, hopes, and fears from the unconscious into the conscious, where we can make use of the information. And if we allow the outer world to inform us in our process, we receive inspiration, comfort, support, and additional material with which to work. The spiral of body, emotions, and mind, together with the inner/outer pulsation of attention, offers us a grounded and embodied awareness of our experience. Speaking of questions, isn't this full aliveness what we really want from life?

Wendy Palmer is a fourth-degree black belt in aikido and the author of *The Intuitive Body*. For focusing on one's inner growth, she suggests we ask a question such as "What quality would be beneficial for me right now?" When an answer arises — say, for example, "tenderness" — she then asks, "If there were more tenderness in my being, what would that feel like?"

Two things happen with Palmer's kind of question. One, she opens space for an original insight in response to the question. Two, Palmer draws to herself the "feeling" of her request. This makes the question more than a mental activity; it now involves the emotions and the body sensations. All of the self is present and alert to this question. And all of the inner resources of self are present and alert as source material for the answer. Palmer says, "Asking questions shifts our attention to the state of wonder, the place where our creativity and intuition arise."

Tracking Down Truth

We all have the same body and the same senses and live on the same planet with brown dirt and blue sky. But each one of us perceives this world through our own body and senses. Each one of us, therefore, *produces entirely original stories stemming from each of our own particular lives.*

We write to discover these gifts, and we write to offer these gifts to others through our own authentic voices. We listen for our trueness word by word. Michael Jones, pianist and author of *Creating the Imaginative Life,* says that in order to find his voice while writing music, he played one note at a time, over and over again, listening for authenticity. Although this was very slow work, he said he finally grasped a sense of his own connection to life and his unique expression of it. He believes that as soon as we open to imagination, we open ourselves to new channels of inflowing data.

When we open to imagination, we are, in effect, asking a question. We are creating those new channels of inflowing data with the expression of our curiosity. We come alive when we ask ourselves: "What would that feel like? How did that happen? Why did I do this?" And we track the answer through our sensory experience and our bodies as well as our minds. I've found my car keys by recalling how my hand felt the last time I held those keys. The sensation arose, then the image of where I was standing. I returned to that spot and discovered my keys there. My conscious mind was unaware of where I'd put the keys, but another part of me held the knowledge and informed me.

In my work, I've used a piñata as a metaphor for a wasp nest. Originally, the metaphor occurred to me as a flash of connection. I could have attributed that flash to luck or the muse; I chose instead to track down its source. The key pieces for me were body movement, my senses, and an emotion. I recalled seeing a little boy hop away and cringe after he swatted at a pink-and-white crepe-paper donkey hanging from a tree limb. I tied that image to my memory of once tentatively poking at a fallen wasp nest. The body movements of both the little boy and myself expressed fear about what we might have been provoking. And on both occasions, I was aware of autumn aromas and the warmth of sunshine. These two images mated in my mind to become the metaphor.

Scientifically, that's how it works: senses trigger memory held in the body. None of this would have been noticed or captured in my consciousness if I hadn't written it down. Years later, I used the metaphor in my novel *Crybaby Ranch*.

CHAPTER FIVE

Nature as a Writing Partner

NATURE IS OUR FIRST MOTHER AND OUR FIRST LOVE, our first teacher in the lessons of life and the lessons of death. Native Americans offer newly born children a ceremony called Touch the Earth to acknowledge this relationship. At the time of my first grandson's birth, I didn't know about this custom; I only knew I felt the urge to perform such a ceremony. Soon after Coulter's birth, I took him outside, sat on the ground with him in my lap, and reached his tiny hand to touch the grassy earth. I announced to us both, "This is the first time Coulter Buhler touches the earth." It felt good and has served as a precedent for our relationship. Coulter is now eighteen; through the years, we have spent time together alongside creeks and lakes and on the mountain trails.

Friendly with Nature

Many of us began life not with an intimate relationship with the outdoors but rather with an antagonistic one. In the minds of my parents and their parents, nature was a force from which they should protect themselves and their children. Animals, bugs, cold, heat, wind, and dirt invaded their homes, attacked their comfort, spurred illness. It wasn't until the next generation that we began to camp out during vacations with our children and consider gardening a hobby rather than a chore.

Deepening our relationship with nature teaches us much about understanding our own creative energy. Tanya Wilkinson says in her book *Medea's Folly*, "Nature renews life by taking life apart. The fundamental regeneration of life depends on the disintegration of life." Organic materials decay and break down into parts that produce fertile soil. This is the pattern for the process of naming, detailing, and interacting. We are taking ourselves and nature apart, getting conscious of them both piece by piece. We are opening the pods, counting the seeds, fingering the edges of a leaf, smelling dirt, chewing grass stems, listening to wind. And inside, we are journeying to our instinctive center, the reptile brain.

Nature is the macrocosm; we are the microcosm. Nature is our parent and guide, offering the pattern for our own creativity and, even more, offering itself as a source for our revitalization. We take in what our senses bring us; we give out what our bodies and emotions feel, and there we are: living at a higher level of consciousness and producing honest writing for our creative and healing use.

There was a time when doctors used to send patients to the mountains or desert when no other cure succeeded. I still believe in this remedy. When completely exhausted, I revert: I hunt and gather. Go straight to the woods and pick berries, collect pinecones in a basket, track animals. Walk the beach and pocket shells, wade in the creek and stack rocks. This kind of unified mind/body/soul experience cannot be duplicated by any other activity. Even hiking or skiing involves a destination, a sense of achievement, a purpose. But aimlessly following the tracks of an elk in snow or eating wild strawberries found while meandering in a meadow involves a kind of giving over of one's purposeful self to the earth.

The journey begins when the senses open to the natural world. Tuning in to nature's aliveness awakens the instinctive body. This awakening stirs emotion, and emotion in turn attaches itself to memories, hopes, fears, and dreams, bringing them into conscious awareness. In short, nature triggers our stories.

The act of writing, moving pen across paper, integrates mind, body, and spirit. When I write outdoors, my experience of nature becomes an exchange with my inner self, and I create an awareness of belonging to the great chain of life. Writing becomes an experience of grounding myself and of unearthing my stories. The body itself guides us through the natural order in which we take in data, relate to it, and give it back out.

To summarize the path: Our first receptors are the five senses, which alert the reptile brain. We name what our senses report to us, and the data enters the midbrain and arouses emotion stored in the body. As we describe an object from the natural world, we create a relationship with it as well as making associations from our memories and dreams as the data interacts in the neocortex.

Now we are exchanging exquisite awareness with the natural world around us as the senses pull in the earth's aliveness, which in turn stirs our own. In this alerted, awakened state, our stories rise from the unconscious to the conscious. These stories are used for our creative writing or for our personal healing.

Near-Death Experience

The writer C Diane Ealy suggests that just as a plant must die and go to seed in order for new plants to grow, so, too, must the creator. She says the creator dies a bit with each creation "at the deepest levels of creativity...yet at the end of the entire process the person is reborn a more whole, mature person." So you could say that what we're after here is a near-death experience...without the near-death part.

This process of conscious awareness offers an experience that guides each of us to our own truth, a clearing of the blocks to aliveness. In reports of near-death experiences, people often have the sensation of leaving their body during a traumatic moment, then reentering with profound changes in their outlook and an enhanced quality of perceiving life. Most of us have already left the body to one degree or another, living in a state of detachment from it. Our culture teaches us to experience our body from the outside, not the inside. For example, we often step outside ourselves to view how we measure up to our own or others' expectations. So now we start at the point of reentering our body, but more deeply than ever before. We do this through alerting our senses and allowing the three-step process of a Spirit Walk to carry us into an awakening of self and place. The same results occur in near-death experiences: we undergo a profound change of outlook and enjoy an enhanced quality of life. An alignment occurs with a system of intelligence greater than our own. We engage in life as a participant, rather than as a spectator. We realize that we are part of the unfolding of life, that our listening to birdsong is the other half of the bird's singing it, that witnessing the unfurling of a wave or a leaf is partnering with the water or the tree. The numinous light of understanding so often reported in near-death experiences need not be saved for the end of the dark tunnel.

Law of Opposites

The Kybalion is an ancient Egyptian book of philosophy written by sages known as the Three Initiates, who, legend claims, planted the first seeds of wisdom on earth. The book lists seven universal laws, one of which states that there are no opposites; instead, the two poles of an idea move by degrees along a continuum from one end of the spectrum to the other. For example, there is not a point at which cold water turns into hot. The same is true of poor and rich, night and day, young and old — there is not one point at which the switch occurs, but rather it occurs by degrees, moving bit by bit from one end point to the other.

So if this idea of becoming alert to life — "relentlessly present," as Deena Metzger phrases it — in our everyday awareness seems too big a job, realize that the only thing required is to move by degrees, bit by bit, toward this way of being.

Sometimes I suspect that the system of life is contained by this law and that the idea with which each of us comes into the world is to move toward our opposite, with the goal of achieving balance. Another way of saying that might be to die to our old selves, as the mystics phrase it, or to dismantle ourselves into our separate pieces, as we discussed happens in nature, and then put ourselves back together again. This, too, may be the purpose of near-death experiences, a sort of psychic dismantling down to the separate pieces and a reorganizing of the soul.

I was once an indecisive, dependent woman who leaned excessively on her husband. For me, it was the process of writing that continually threw me back into myself, because only *I* could decide what to write. I learned to depend on a flow of original feelings and ideas, and eventually, I loved writing so much that I designed my life around it, whereas once I had designed my life around my husband. Writing ultimately altered me as a person and challenged every one of my relationships, as well as my basic value system. For the first time in my life, I wanted something just for myself, rather than doing what made everyone else happy. The necessity of making creative decisions by myself turned me into an independent thinker. As a result, I was no longer a woman without definition, and not everybody liked the new me. That demanded further independence from me or else a total capitulation back into my old self, which would mean giving up writing. A thing I could no longer do.

Many writers discover similar patterns at work in their lives. By writing our truth, we move ourselves from one pole to the opposite pole, degree by degree. The result is that we discover our own personal point of balance along the continuum.

When my son Toby was ten, he became outraged by the elephant poachers in Africa and vowed that when he grew up, he was going to become a law enforcer and arrest them all. The next week, he thought instead that maybe he'd become a poacher himself because they made lots of money selling the ivory. He was testing the edges of the law of opposites, moving along the continuum. Happily, I can report that Toby grew up to become a police officer. Even so, his life revolves around the central idea of crime, and so do the lives of the criminals he arrests. They are operating at opposing polar degrees, which makes it possible for one to turn into the other. In fact, this is our hope when we punish criminals and our fear when we offer power to our protectors.

Using this law of opposites is also how we open imaginatively to writing and to self-knowledge, allowing the unexpected to occur. We, too, can move degree by degree, and in time we learn to make leaps in thought from one extreme to the other in our writing and in our life choices. This movement along the continuum is the anatomy of story; it's how surprise works, as well as humor, drama, and mystery. It is the means for widening the spectrum of life's possibilities. Writers can cultivate ways of inviting the unexpected; we can learn to take leaps.

In reading the best memoirs, we are drawn to the story of how the narrator began in one place and ended in another. Mary Karr, author of *The Liars' Club* and two follow-up memoirs, tells the story of transforming from a teenage druggie to a poet and bestselling author. She began in this story as a person numbing to life and moved to being someone excruciatingly alert. Karr became her opposite.

We use this same law of opposites as writers of fiction. The characters that move from one end of the spectrum to the opposite end tell the stories that fully engage us. In a romance, for instance, we set our two lovers in opposition to one another, then move them by degrees from their positions of dislike to like, or from indifference to caring, or from strangers to intimates, or from singles to married partners. Often, when we write, we have other characters moving from likable to despicable, from strong to weak, or from success to failure. In part, this is the job of each writer: to take a character or situation and turn it into its opposite in a believable manner; it will be convincing only if we move the reader degree by degree through our story.

In my novel *Crybaby Ranch*, for example, I needed to write about a father who was irritating. I only knew my own father well enough to write about at length, but I wanted the freedom that comes when you write about a stranger. Besides, I didn't want my dad harmed by my novel (or — as he often joked — for him to cut me out of his will). I discovered that if I wrote about a father who was motivated by reasons *opposite* from my own father's motivations, many characteristics carried over and resulted in the same effects. The interesting part, as well as the educational part, was thinking through the idea of what exactly would be the opposite of my father.

I worked with a particular quality that defined the father character in my story: his controlling nature. My own father was always early. If he was due to visit me in Jackson Hole in August, I'd suspect him of lurking around the valley in July. When he did arrive, he'd say he was going to pick me up for dinner at 7:00 PM, and he'd be honking his horn in my driveway at 6:15. In my novel, I created the father as a character who was always late. It turned out this father was still familiar to me and a stinker, in just the way I needed him to be. He was always holding people up, making them rush; he was irritating, frustrating, dominating. This worked because these two opposites — being late and being early — revolve around the central idea of time, in this case, controlling time. I succeeded in creating a character who was not recognizable as my father (keeping me safely in the will) and yet who acted from an identical need to control situations and people. I had experience with this character, and I could write honestly about him.

In writing for purposes of personal expansion, working with opposites is an enlightening exercise. As in the father example above, once I pulled out a single characteristic and determined its opposite, I understood things about my father and myself that I hadn't seen before. During much of my time with my father, I felt I wasn't measuring up. I was never ready when he wanted me to be, for one. Once I flipped the quality to its opposite, the underlying motivations became clear. I got that pleasing my father, or measuring up, wasn't in the cards. He had long ago determined that his job was to keep me on my toes, and so he continued to stretch his expectations above my head, even in the small ways of urging me to scurry around trying to get ready for dinner ahead of time.

Consider addressing a single quality of a parent or partner, and go through the process of figuring out what the opposite of that quality may be. Write how it plays out in the relationship between the two of you. Nice surprises may surface.

Thinking in terms of opposites and moving from one pole to the other by degrees increases the agility of our minds. A wider array of options is suddenly available to us in our creative work as well as our personal lives. I learned something valuable writing about the fictional father. After completing *Crybaby Ranch*, when my father and I set up dates, I told him, "I will not be late, but neither will I be early, not one minute." I took back control of my time.

Nature is filled with opposites, and we need to acknowledge them with our writing. Light and dark are two sticks, and the friction created between them bursts into the flame of creative energy.

CHAPTER SIX

Going Deeper

WE NEED NOT BE AFRAID TO LOOK CLOSELY at the source of our power and creative energy, nor to diagram it as we might diagram the life of a plant, breaking it down into its separate parts: seeds, roots, sprouts, blossoms. We don't need to squinch up with closed eyes and just hope a blossom occurs when we sit down with paper and pen. If a blossom occurs — an insight, a poem — that's satisfying, but so is casting seeds, producing roots, and developing sprouts. And if any of those parts isn't going well, it's also okay to look at the process closely and use our body, mind, and spirit to detect just where the depletion of nutrients is occurring.

We offer our attention, we form a question, we hold open the space for an answer. And then we move degree by degree toward our intention.

Our authority rests within, not without, dependent only on ourselves.

Here's the pathway we're following:

1. Name the information your senses bring you from the natural world. Use all five senses: sight, sound, touch, taste, and smell. List your perceptions in writing.
2. Detail one thing in the outdoors in a full written description, again using all five senses. Include your body sensations and comfort level.
3. Interact with your outdoor surroundings to allow your awareness of nature and your presence in it to bring your emotions into consciousness. Write down the responses that occur in your body. Allow your memories, hopes, fears, and dreams to arise. Write them down.

Name

When we name what we receive through our senses, we alert ourselves to be more present in our surroundings. It's a gentle knock on the door of our attention and bodies. The list we generate as we write down what we see, hear, touch, taste, and smell becomes raw material for creative use, and the act of writing grounds us to this place and this time.

Our senses are the power lines that connect our body to the earth.

There is no wrong way to do this. Make a list of the things around you. Make it as long or short as you like. Some days I have to stay in place and make a very long list before I feel myself absorbing the reality of being outdoors, in my body, paying attention to life. Some days I make a quick run through all five senses and bound through the woods so present inside my skin and on my planet that I feel as if I am backlit and glowing like a rose petal.

The idea is to offer your attention to yourself and the planet you live on. All living things flourish with attention. Attention is a form of prayer. Studies have shown that offering your attention to weak plants, pets, or people is an act of healing, no matter how far away the object of your attention resides. So I imagine that giving attention to our own body and the land we stand upon heals more than most of us think.

In response to the terrorist attacks of September 11, 2001, President Bush told a story about a four-year-old girl puzzled by how the terrorists could hate a whole country. She said, "Why don't we just tell them our names?" Even she knew the importance of naming, that once a person or a thing has a name, it becomes noble, sacred, unique.

In *Writing Down the Bones*, Natalie Goldberg discusses the difference in her experience of walking down the street noticing trees versus walking down the street with a tree guide in her hand, noticing elms, oaks, maples. Naming the trees distinguished her experience of seeing each uniquely shaped leaf and the shadow it cast, touching the bark, and enjoying the fragrance. The act of naming seems elementary, and of course it is; yet this does not in any way diminish its importance. That it is elementary means it opens itself to easy use. Name what you see, hear, touch, taste, and smell, and your experience of life expands and deepens. Write this down and you own it, body, mind, and soul.

As an example of how naming works in everyday life, I think of my oldest friend, Gloria, who sent me a thank-you note for a beaded necklace I made for her. Though Gloria is not a writer, this note she sent is luminous with the simplicity of good writing and pure feeling, and what Gloria did was name. She named each part of the necklace in her note, so that I knew she shared my creative experience of making the necklace for her.

And I then shared her experience of receiving it. Here's a bit of Gloria's note: "Your favorite bead with the flowers is mine, too. But then the bison feels so smooth, and I like the blue bead with the caps. The silver clasp on the necklace is elegant. I enjoy the sensory pleasure of feeling each bead." When in doubt about how to write a thank-you note, take Gloria's lead and name what your senses experienced.

When I hike or snowshoe with my friend Bette, she settles into her gear, then stills. Softly, she names the things around her: sagebrush, rabbitbrush, rock outcropping, chickadee song, orange lichen, wind, lodgepole pine. "I smell elk," she may say, or "Feel that sunshine on your cheeks?" She told me once about snowshoeing alone into the trees, past a family of moose, to eat her lunch on the shore of the Gros Ventre River. Bette sat on a log and took herself through all five senses, naming what she was experiencing and giving her attention for several moments to each sensory activity. "It was a wonderful day. I'll never forget that lunch." Because Bette pays such deep attention to her experiences outdoors, she makes surprising discoveries: the claw marks of a grizzly bear on an aspen tree or wolf tracks as large as her hand in the snow. Her log home is filled with abandoned birds' nests and baskets of dried rose hips; rocks and feathers grace the bay window where she has breakfast in the morning. Bette came to the outdoors late in life, and now in her midsixties, she covers the Tetons on foot all year long, hiking or skiing many miles each day. That afternoon on the shore of the Gros Ventre, she suddenly noticed a newly made path down the cut bank across the river. The snow was smeared with the reddish clay dirt brought up from the riverbank, showing it had recent use. As she watched, a wolf appeared on the high bank across the river, then another and another. She sat in silence and watched the wolves cross the ridge, a pack that no one even knew had traveled that far from Yellowstone at the time.

Journals are a good place for naming, creating lists of any kind. Don't hesitate to write your grocery list or to-do list in your journal. Your lists tell much about where you are at any given moment in your life.

After September 11, we often heard people say in TV interviews that never again would they start their day without watching the sun rise and listening to the birds sing. People surviving trauma or threat to their lives, whether it's a personal or a nationwide event, often feel an immediate appreciation for the earth and the beloved people in their lives.

In short, many survivors greet life anew and go after more of a conscious experience of living. People engaged with creative energy also need and desire this daily awareness of their connection to the earth. So begin your day naming what your senses bring you, and you'll find this simple exercise enhances your experience of connection to self and earth. It's important to move beyond just a mental or spiritual connection. Writing your list pulls your body in, making the experience a full event, from sensory awareness through your body into a physical product. A full-circle event.

Detail

When you take something from the natural world and describe it in detail, use all of your senses and body sensations.

Here's an example of detailing from my friend Hannah Hinchman's journal, published under the title *A Trail through*

Leaves: "Thirty-seven below zero last night. No vehicles will start. Magpies have a rim of ice around their eyes." I think of this often when the mercury in my own thermometer shrivels into a red pearl and the magpies sit inside the shelter of the Engelmann spruce outside my window. Imagine the pleasure of noticing such detail. Hannah is good at this. She pays attention, and she records what she discovers in her journal. She began writing them as a teenager and now has a collection of dozens of black hardbound journals. Once she wrote, "How do moose cross ice? On the pointed tips of their hooves." To get this information, she did more than wait and watch. She created an intimate relationship with the object of her attention.

Naming and describing organize the senses and the information that rushes toward us. Often, when I feel excitement over something and want desperately to remember the particulars, I nearly numb out with the overload of emotion and information. If I try to take in the whole picture, I can't recall anything meaningful, only the general outlines of the event. So my story and my memory are flattened by a lack of detail.

For example, one winter night, hours after I'd gone to sleep, my pup, Tess, began barking. She didn't go to the front of the house or even the bedroom door; she stood before my tall bedroom windows and barked so hard her front paws lifted off the floor. I tiptoed out of bed, afraid of what I might see — an escaped convict prying open my window came to mind. I peeked out of the edge of the heavy velvet drapery that keeps out subzero drafts. There, inches from the window glass, was a mother moose and her young, leggy twins. They were eating the rose hips that grow wild in a tangle with the willows beside my window. At first, I was filled with wonder and couldn't take it all in. But then I slowed myself and did a mental Spirit Walk right there. I named what my senses brought to my attention: red berries capped with snow, chomping sounds, chilled bare feet, too cold to smell anything, too excited to taste anything. Still, I did pretty well, and next I began to notice details. My reward: I saw snowflakes in the eyelashes of the mother moose. If I hadn't broken my experience down into its separate pieces, I never would have seen that while trying to take in the whole wonderful event of moose in my yard.

After a while, Mama lay down in the snow beside the willows. Her twins lay down next to her. I dragged open the drapes to expose the whole width of window and went back to bed. From my pillows, I could see the three of them, sleeping in the snow, dreaming moose dreams. I fell asleep with the same kind of contentment I remember from childhood when crawling into bed with my grandparents in the night.

In writing description, we needn't be fancy. Plain and simple is good. Another example from Hannah's journal: "Admiring the sharp tips of the spruces." Nice. Brings us to the present moment. Noting even what we consider the obvious, such as the sharp tips of spruces, is poetic because our minds often skip over acknowledging such things. Both the writer and the reader are brought to the immediate sense of aliveness in this place, this moment, with this simple observation, using plain words.

We seek clarity. Even people intent on addiction and distraction, I believe, would trade in their numbness for clarity, for a mind as tidy and organized as a California Closet, those advertised units with a cubbyhole and rack for every item. I once thought paradox and confusion were two hindrances to clear thinking, or even faults within myself. I thought I had to solve the paradoxes and clear away the confusion. Then I discovered that the two stone dogs guarding many Buddhist temples represented Paradox and Confusion. Amazing. Honored with sculptures. What a relief to learn that I could embrace these states of mind. I embrace them now by acknowledging and describing them until I have a relationship with them that includes the awareness that I don't understand everything about them. Isn't this how relationships work with our mates and friends and even children? We don't understand everything about them, yet our desire and aim are to live with them in peace and comfort.

Interact

Once we have named and detailed, settled into our bodies and placed ourselves on the earth, physically exchanging awareness with nature, capturing it in words on paper, we are engaged in interacting with the life force, and our inner being rises to the surface, bringing with it our emotions and our memories, hopes, and fears. These are our stories. Write them down.

Like waking dreams, emerging stories are full of the symbols of our life. In time, as we collect these stories, we may discover themes, repeating images, characters playing the same roles but wearing different disguises. Watch how these stories from the past find correspondence in your present day, how similar characters may show up again and symbols reappear. Consider synchronicity your teacher. This is similar to reading a text with certain information offered in bold type and underlined.

If you write to create, you experience stress as well as flow and need a therapy of sorts to address the stress. Chances are you look to journal keeping — writing — for that. If you use writing as your therapy, chances are you are also interested in producing creative nonfiction or fiction. Therapeutic writing and creative writing are natural partners and will support and enhance each other.

Invite nature into the process. Nature is a born healer and a teacher of creative energy. What happens when nature participates in the process is the same thing that happens when you take on a supporting partner or loving guide. You share the burden, you pull in a cooperative system, you are no longer out there swinging without direction, swirling in a vicious circle of words. With nature nothing is forced; effort is not helpful. You step outside and engage your senses. Nature and your body take it from there.

Throughout this book, two strands of experience prevail. One strand is an awareness of fully inhabiting place: you stand on this earth, this mountaintop, in this weedy field, school yard, city park; the sky is above, the land is below. You stand among trees, grasses, weeds, rocks, sand dunes, insects, birds, small mammals. The second strand of experience is the awareness of self. You are in your skin, supported by bone, enabled by muscle. Your senses seek data. Information travels from nature to you, through you, evokes emotion, triggers memory. You braid the two strands together with a third, your writing. Your writing produces a tangible product and again becomes two strands of experience: one is creating, one is healing.

Creating and healing are soul work, soil work.

I believe we all have to do this work of bringing the unconscious into our consciousness. If we don't, life has a way of
doing it for us. Often, we have dug so deeply into our resistance
to the process of becoming conscious that life has to act harshly
just to get our attention.

This is what writing has done for me: it has smoothed away
my resistance and aroused my attention.

I am easy prey for life.

CHAPTER SEVEN

Story of the Body, Body of the Story

NOON AND I AM STILL IN PAJAMAS. I rinse out my coffee cup, cast eyes up to the kitchen clock, and say out loud, "You're a slob. Nobody hangs around in their pajamas till lunchtime." Then I catch myself. I can do what I feel like, and I didn't feel like getting dressed this morning. "Always finding fault," I admonish. "Give yourself credit sometimes."

That's two reprimands in as many seconds. I catch myself, take a big breath, and ask my body: "What do you want now?" I am trying to learn to bring my body into awareness.

Most of us spend our lives unconscious to physical messages, sometimes deliberately numbing them out, because we have the idea that doing so is the most intelligent way to live. As far as our awareness is concerned, the head and spirit are mostly unattached to the body, as if all that is meaningful stops at the neck. Below the neck is like the Thunder Basin grasslands on the map of Wyoming: a big blank spot. We drive around this spot (no state roads cut through it), just as in our conscious awareness map, we often drive around the area below the neck. Both the body and Thunder Basin are wildlands with intelligent life and their own unique beauty, but neither is valued as it should be. We think it is okay to continue engaging our mind and spirit conducting business, playing sports, or pursuing creative projects when our stomach is empty and our bladder is full. It's easy; we just drive around the messages. Sometimes when I'm angry and don't know what to do about it, I say, "I'll just have to swallow that." Push it down into the blank spot.

Recently, I acted on information from the results of a blood test that showed an off-the-charts thyroid hormone level, which indicated that my thyroid was underactive to the point that I should be experiencing severe physical responses: weakness, frequent infections, muscle and joint pain, to name a few. I didn't believe the test results because I never noticed any of the ten major symptoms. Never noticed.

In my head, I was full of ideas and plans, enthusiasm and anticipation, and never involved other parts of my being that might wish to offer input. I was acting like the activities director of a cruise ship, one who refused to notice that the travelers were too tired to play one more game, too constipated to partake of one more banquet, too weak to pull the lever of another slot machine, and were infecting each other with contagious germs at the compulsory ballroom dances. Besides that, the ship itself was slowly losing power. While I was madly corralling the troops for another volleyball game on the upper deck, the very ship itself — my life — was sinking farther and farther below the waterline. I hadn't *noticed* yet, but I was cancelling meetings, backing out of gatherings with friends, and beginning to have a hard time fulfilling my work schedule.

After I began taking the medication, I realized that I had

experienced quite a few of the hypothyroid symptoms, but I had been too numb to my body to be aware of them. Around this time, I read Marion Woodman's wonderful book *Bone*, a journal of the year in which she struggled with cancer. She discussed her own realization that her mind and spirit soared ahead, leaving her poor body behind to deal with the practicalities of life on earth without her awareness or support. Nice to know I was not alone. That's when I vowed: from this time forward, I am honoring the body wisdom that I believe was pushed down below the neck and not given voice.

So here I am in my pajamas, at noon, asking my body, "What would you like now?"

I can't believe it. My body wants a bubble bath.

"It's noon," I repeat out loud. But, really, it sounds good. The thermometer on my log cabin porch says zero degrees; a wind begins to howl. Clearly, that predicted snowstorm is right on time. I run hot water, pour in bubbling soap, light three vanilla candles and set them on the tub's edge, then lower myself into the steam.

One reason we fail to eat properly or take bathroom breaks is anxiety about time. A bubble bath with candlelight presents just the remedy for that, because as we consciously inhabit our body, we inhabit present time. It is impossible to be in the body and worry about the future in the same moment.

I feel the warm steam loosen my facial muscles. I drop my attention down below my face and into my chest and stomach, hips and feet. I feel myself fully embodied.

Suddenly, my eyes well up with tears, and my chest fills with a feeling of nostalgia. But this emotion doesn't make sense. Nostalgia? I let go of the need for logic and allow the tears to flow, my chest to heave with this strange feeling.

Like returning to Grandma's house, I am reinhabiting a place I haven't been since childhood.

Returning Home

Nostalgia in Greek: "returning home."

Many of us have been homesick for our own body. Somehow, we don't think we are supposed to want such a thing and, like eating dessert first, don't think we are supposed to give in to the desire. Desire, many of us have learned, is dangerous when it comes to the body. Desire from the body leads to no good, our culture suggests.

As children, we are taught not to touch ourselves in certain places while in public, one of those places being quite prominent on our face — our nose. "Get your finger out of your nose." I heard it as a child, I said it as a parent, and I now hear my children tell their children. Without recommending that we pick our nose in public, I do wish to encourage pleasure in our physical sensations, including desire.

Desire is a body event. It is irrational; it scares us. We have no mental control over what we do or do not desire; therefore, to a controlling mind or society, the only way out is to diminish the importance of the body and its sensations. However, to a curious mind seeking truth, the body offers information untainted by anything but actual experience.

The body never lies.

Body as Warehouse

The body is where we store our unacknowledged grief, pain, sadness, regret, misery. Because of this, we don't always want to go there. Many of us consider negative emotions to be not useful but rather waste material from unpleasant events we prefer to forget. We dump this waste in the place we don't understand and don't value, just as our government dumps shiploads of the country's waste into the ocean and sends trainloads of nuclear waste to parts of the West — to those last remaining frontiers not valued as real estate. We humans dump our waste — what we don't know what to do with — into our unconscious, where our bodies, instead of our consciousness, express it.

Poet David Whyte says there is no way we can follow ourselves to our desires without opening up to our grief. Whyte's poem "Well of Grief" says, "Those who will not slip beneath the still surface on the well of grief... will never find the source from which we drink."

Being in our body is the first level of awareness of life. Acknowledging comfort or unease and taking action on the body's behalf honors our inner wisdom. This is how we recycle our "wastes" into creative energy. In writing, we acknowledge our body's sensations, follow the awareness to the emotions that rise, and capture the stories that come. In this way, we imitate nature by maintaining renewable resources, as a tree does when it fertilizes itself with its fallen leaves. And like a tree that has rings of growth telling of past droughts, good rains, and fires, we also hold layers and layers of stories within our bodies.

During a deep-tissue massage, my sister, Gayle, experienced images and memories that flashed as fast as a flickering movie screen, while the therapist worked different parts of her aching body. People losing a lot of weight often report that, as layers of tissue are released and they spiral through their past shapes, the accompanying emotions are often replayed. If we consciously retrieve our stories from their warehouse in our bodies, can we aid our body's comfort and health?

Dr. Christiane Northrup, author of *Women's Bodies, Women's Wisdom*, connects the word *restore*, when talking about healing our bodies, to the idea of re-storying, or retelling our stories. She recognizes that the restoration of our health and our energy is deeply related to acknowledging our stories. She believes we have control over our lives and physical health through acknowledgment and expression of these stories.

One of the first things I noticed when becoming aware of my body was that I habitually curled the toes of my right foot. I swear, my shoe size leaped a whole number once I began to relax those toes. Even now, it's one of the first signs telling me that I'm anxious. When I stand above a ski slope and try to decide whether or not it's too steep for me to ski and my toes are curled, I know I better sidestep downhill a ways.

My feet tell stories when I give them the chance. One story is a childhood memory of my family joking about my big feet. Then, when I was eleven, I accidentally stepped on a baby chick that had been my pet. Fuzzy with cream-colored down one moment and bleeding beneath my big foot the next. I've curled my toes over that for dozens of years.

My father took on the serious task of toughening his children for the real world. He teased me unmercifully about stepping on my baby chick and kept it up until Alzheimer's took his memory hostage. Toughening was his gift to his children, and I often thank him for it; yet I have had some unraveling to do in order to balance this toughening with equal parts of tendering. But then my father, too, had some balancing work to do. My father came late to emotions. Only in his eighties, after years of caring for my mother, who had Alzheimer's before him, could he hug his children and let us witness his tears or failures.

Loving both parents as they have suffered through Alzheimer's disease, one following the other, has motivated me to look deeply into this word *remember*, defined as "being mindful." *Member* comes from the Latin root *membrum*, meaning "flesh" or "body part." This suggests that being mindful includes acknowledging the "waste material" we have stuffed down into our body. To "re-member" is to reclaim our body.

If our intention is to sew our heads back onto our bodies, we must give up the belief that our heads are the only place in which we receive information or process experience.

"There is a brain in the bowel, however inappropriate that concept might seem to be," says Michael D. Gershon in *The Second Brain*. The notion of "gut reaction," of "knowing in my gut," is on the mark. Serotonin, a mood regulator in the brain, functions as a neurotransmitter in the bowel, and 95 percent of serotonin is produced in the bowel.

Try This

You've been asked today, "How are you?" Maybe you answered, "Fine." Maybe you lied. The body experiences discomfort with lies. To name a few changes, muscles stiffen, digestive juices alter, and — this is how lie detectors work — pulse rates become erratic and sweat glands overproduce. Your body dislikes lies. Tell the truth now. Write a paragraph or list describing a general awareness of comfort or discomfort in your body. Name your sensations. "Chilled, restless, achy, antsy, sluggish, tired." Describe the most prominent sensation in detail. At any point where you become stuck, tune your awareness in to your senses. Follow the sensory information that most interests you. When stories arise, write them down. In this way, we bring the information to the surface of consciousness. Often, that's all that is necessary to ease discomfort.

If we are willing to lie to a stranger who's asking how we are today, how do we respond to people we know? Write down what you do to please others — your mate, children, coworkers, boss, friends — that you really don't want to do. Take one thing on the list that attracts your attention and ask yourself, "What feelings do I cut off or override to do this thing?"

We may choose to please others because we believe our true selves are unlovable. Ask yourself, "How am I unlovable?" Write down what occurs to you.

Marion Woodman says, "As I go deeper, I realize that the voice that says, 'I'm unlovable' is in the cells. Therefore, it's at the cellular level that transformation has to take place."

She also says, "We try to push all the parts of ourselves that are unacceptable down into hiding in our bodies." Begin to pull those parts back up into the open now.

———

The Soft Body

Our culture values a "hard body" and uses the term in advertisements for exercise equipment and diet products, and uses young, hard bodies as models in advertising almost everything else.

But what we really need for entering life fully is a soft body. A soft body allows itself to be penetrated by life; it remains open, accessible, receptive, available to the present moment, and agile in responding to events. A soft body is poised for a relationship with the world around us.

When we wake up in the morning, we are soft and warm, still in the grip of our nightlong relaxation. Then, as we move into our day, we begin to assume a kind of armor; muscles harden as thoughts come to mind about the jobs we need to accomplish, the lack of time in which to do them, and the problems we will face. By the time we turn the knob for our morning shower, muscles are hard, the spine stiff, movements inept. But when we keep in the present moment, enjoy our body awakening, and notice what our senses bring us about the new day outside, our body stays soft, our movements nimble.

Writing student Carrie says she tries to keep her body soft throughout the day but often discovers wooden upper arms or iron cords in her neck at her office job, and then she reminds herself to resume softness. Some days she does well; most days, she says, she forgets all about it by three in the afternoon as she rushes to finish up her work. "Then all I want to do in the evening is recover," Carrie says. "Have a glass of wine, dinner, chocolate for dessert, and be stupid on the sofa watching television till bedtime. But those days when I am more successful in keeping soft, I am not content with mindlessness. I have energy to enjoy my free time and often pull out my writing project and work a couple of hours in the evening."

As Mary Oliver says in her poem "Wild Geese," people don't need to promise to be good or to repent on their knees to live fully; they just need "to love the soft animal of the body and do what it loves."

What does the soft animal of the body love? It loves curiosity, passion, ease. It loves its own rhythms. It loves play and work, rest and movement, comfortable clothes, good food, clean water, the outdoors.

A soft body dislikes hurry, stress, and exercise only for the sake of burning calories or building muscle. It dislikes driven activity, restrictive clothing, and stale food, water, air, ideas.

A soft body loves to sleep when it's tired, wake when it's refreshed; eat when it's hungry, abstain when it's not; drink when it's thirsty. It loves the feel of its own skin, stretching its muscles, moving rhythmically. A soft body loves itself.

Honoring the Body

When Ella was a child, her mother would ask, after Ella had been in the bathtub on her own for a while, "Did you wash your body?" That meant did Ella remember to use soap and water to wash the areas usually covered by her underwear and never to be touched in public. During Ella's first day at school, the teacher, Miss Adams, announced in health class that they'd talk about the *body*, and Ella's face heated up and turned as bright as the red wool skirt and vest her mother had dressed her in.

This is an extreme version of how our culture has viewed bodies in the past. But we didn't talk about them or heed them or give them much awareness; it was as if we were so busy trying to separate ourselves from the animal kingdom that we wanted to admit no connection whatsoever to anything we may have in common with animals: elimination, illness, female cycles, birth, and death. When we moved beyond this, we leaped into another form of dishonoring the body, one that values mostly how the body looks to others, how well it compares to current fashion. Though ads may flash on TV for solutions to the social faux pas of flatulence, heavy menstrual periods, and incontinence, an embarrassed silence still falls into a room when a person admits to a life-threatening illness, the same way it once did when our grandmothers announced their pregnancies. And some continue to ask where the "little girl's room" or "little boy's room" is located, as if we must regress to children before admitting our bodies need relief.

The truth is most of us pay more attention to our clothes than we do to our bodies. We'll tend our shoes before we'll tend our feet. Yet our bodies are our libraries, holders of our reference material, our body wisdom. We need to read our bodies.

CHAPTER EIGHT

The Body Never Lies

ATTENTION IS DIRECTED ENERGY. When we direct energy toward ourselves, we hold within our awareness a vast network of activity. This network needs organization in order for us to absorb the information our being holds. Our goal is to create a relationship with ourselves that includes input from all parts.

Three Centers of Awareness

To simplify our view, it helps to divide our attention into three centers of awareness: body, emotion, and mind. These three centers correspond to the three parts of the triune brain: reptile, midbrain, and neocortex. And to the three parts of the Spirit Walk path: naming, describing, and interacting.

Along with separating the experience into three areas of concentration — body, emotions, mind — I suggest we also assign each area a word, a verbal magnet, that draws our attention to the particular center. Our consciousness also needs a physical place on our being that represents each center, and a question to aid in concentrating our awareness on the center.

65

Body Center

The body center concentrates on the physical organization of our being: our senses, our body systems, our unconscious storage of information, our skin, muscles, bones. The magnet for the body center is *comfort*. This is what the body loves most. Comfort is a simple and clear idea to our bodies. Leisure is comfort; haste is discomfort.

Let's associate the body center with the abdomen, just below the navel. It is a traditional spot in many of the world's religions and philosophies for centering one's awareness. Let's use this question to help ourselves concentrate on the body: "What feels comfortable to me right now?"

Emotion Center

The emotion center concentrates on the feeling activities of our being — our loves and hates and attractions and relationships. The magnet to draw our attention to the emotions is *passion*, and I choose this word because the Latin root for *passion* means "to suffer," yet we also use the word to mean love, and even mindless ardor, as well as fervent concern. For the emotion center, we concentrate attention on the heart, the universal symbol for feeling. The question used to center our attention: "What do I care about right now?"

Mind Center

The mind center concentrates on the thought activities of our being: our curiosities, images, and ideas. For the mind, the word we use as a magnet to draw our attention is *interest*. The mind loves to follow what interests it. Curiosity is its pleasure. We

concentrate attention on the middle of the forehead, also a traditional center in world religions and philosophies. The question:
"What interests me right now?"

The above, arranged in a diagram, looks like this:

	BODY	EMOTION	MIND
Physical center	Lower abdomen	Heart	Forehead
Magnet	Comfort	Passion	Interest
Question	What feels comfortable to me right now?	What do I care about right now?	What interests me right now?
Brain part	Reptile	Midbrain	Neocortex
Spirit Walk	Naming	Describing	Interaction

Energy Knots

The three areas of awareness can work against each other without our realizing it. This, I believe, accounts for our occasional
inability to carry out our intentions and desires. Our emotion
center may want to help our neighbor by babysitting her toddler, yet our body feels tired at the thought, and our mind feels
bored. Some of us push through the other two centers, agree to
the babysitting, and spend a few miserable hours meeting the
needs of our emotion center at the expense of our mental and
physical centers. This creates an energy knot. The flow of our
enthusiasm for life becomes slowed and twisted. And our experience reflects this divisiveness within us.

We are aiming for conscious unity of our entire being. Our goal is to enhance the fullness of our life experience, and this happens more successfully when we are not fragmented in our intentions. Understanding how energy works in our unconscious as expressed by our bodies leads to conscious organization and a unified intent.

Our culture educates us about paying attention to our thoughts but educates us less about minding our emotions, and even less our bodies. Bodies for the most part are overridden. Take two Tylenol, move on. Yet, since our bodies are where the unconscious stores its memory, we want first of all to heed the body and bring the unconscious back into consciousness, in order to live a life of full awareness. To bring what is in the dark into light.

This is the job description of creative writers and journal keepers. We are intent on fully examining what is unconscious for each of us and writing our truth.

In dream imagery, a house often symbolizes our selfhood, the separate rooms symbolizing different parts of us. Using that image of a house, the unconscious represents a control center in the basement that fuels the energy systems. Picture trunks full of photos depicting our stories — past experiences, memories, hopes, and dreams — as the fuel. These photos are fed into this control center to keep the house operating. We may not consciously understand why the lights won't go on in one room, or why they go on but constantly flicker, or why some parts of the house are warm, other parts cold. In other words, why do we fail to create the marriage we have dreamed of yet succeed beyond our dreams in our career — or vice versa? Why are we adept at perceiving dishonesty in people but often fall for poor business deals? It depends on the photos or stories — our memories, teachings, role models, expectations, past experiences — that are fed into the source of our energy. These stories are constantly operating within our field of being, casting light or darkness onto our intentions; either we are conscious of this, or we are working in the dark.

If our thought center wishes to get a degree in economics so that we are assured of job security the rest of our lives, we are not going to succeed unless our emotion and body centers are behind the intention as well. Or we do succeed in getting the degree, and even the career, by a driven will to do so and, in the process, overpower our other centers. While common behavior for many of us, the latter option proves an unsatisfying way to live. The disharmony and frustration that result from such a way of living can only be addressed by numbing out. We numb out the input of two-thirds of our being for the sake of one-third.

For instance, writer Mitchell felt that he could justify the time he spent away from his wife and two daughters writing his novel if he sold it and made money to ease his family's life. The novel didn't sell. He wrote a second novel. When neither novel sold, Mitchell stopped writing. He was miserable because he loved to write. His job as a government employee doing computer work was dull and somewhat stressful, and since he had stopped working on his fiction, his job had become increasingly abrasive to him. Mitchell was considering writing a police procedural novel using stories from his job, because an editor who had rejected his first two novels assured him that such a book would sell. The trouble was that Mitchell couldn't tolerate the idea.

He asked my advice. Should he write the novel an editor

wanted him to write, stop writing altogether, or write the novel he wanted to write — possibly a third novel that wouldn't sell?

Easy. I advised Mitchell to write what he loves. But he also needed to get himself straight about the conflict he had with time. He needed to spend time with both himself and his family. Otherwise, he would be dealing with an energy knot.

If Mitchell ignored his responsibility to address conflicts with his time and energy, he might possibly head toward a future breakdown in the form of disease, depression, addiction, or becoming accident-prone. Certainly he would experience dissatisfaction with his life. And if I were either his wife or daughter, I would feel dissatisfaction with him.

Many writers make bargains with themselves in order to justify time spent writing. One woman wanted to write a novel in the hope of earning respect from her husband's family, who snubbed her work as a salesclerk. Another began a memoir about her son's abuse to pay lawyer fees in order to take the abuser to court. Neither writer had ever published before. In both cases, the writers burdened their creative flow with complex deals with themselves that involved time spent in return for the hope of money or respect earned. This is unnecessary and even subversive. There is a healthier, more honest way.

First, we become aware of the input from each of our three centers by giving expression to them in writing. Next we acknowledge and honor the information gathered. Then we work toward harmonizing the three centers into one intention. We begin with the body.

Let's say an economist, who is working from his mental willpower, finds that physically, his body is restless indoors and feels best when he is active in the outdoors. And yet he likes to create

order out of disorder; the setting of a tidy desk with neatly col-
umned numbers on his computer screen offers comfort. Emotionally, he is unenthusiastic about numbers; rather, he is enthused
by the idea of working with animals. However, his fear for the
future responds to the security that a degree in economics prom-
ises. This person may choose to go ahead with making a living
as an economist and on the side breed and raise show dogs or
pursue some other outdoor involvement with animals. Perhaps
he works with the intention that someday the emphasis will shift
and he will work full-time with animals, knowing that part-time
accounting work can pick up the slack or be resumed full-time
if necessary. These choices can be arrived at with full conscious
awareness, without overriding any parts of ourselves. But it takes
honesty and self-knowledge to arrive at the balance for each of
us, a balance that continually shifts as circumstances change.

Drain or Gain

Before making an important decision, ask yourself this question:
Is this an energy drain or gain?

The Spirit Walk process works well in helping us sort out
our responses. In writing, name your body sensations, emotions,
and any images that come to mind. Choose the sensation, feeling, or image that holds your interest the most or seems to act
like a magnet drawing further information; describe the details
in writing. Next allow the stories to arise. Look for associations.
Do not dismiss memories, emotions, or ideas; they occur at the
moment they do for reasons we must honor whether we understand their appearance or not. Each time we dismiss those things
that occur to us, we belittle our inner voice. Each time we honor
and acknowledge our voice, we strengthen it.

Asking ourselves, "Is this an energy drain or an energy gain?" helps us become conscious of how our energy moves and where it goes, and aware of the rhythm of its flow. We can evaluate our activities, the effect on us of the people around us, and the settings in which we work and play. We do ourselves and others no good if we allow energy drains within our systems. The body tells us the truth. Plain and simple. It's our job to learn to read the gauges: abdomen, heart, and head.

Instead of being whole in our focus or desire to carry out our intentions, we often employ the bird-shot method of directing ourselves toward our goal. It shows our energy is scattered when we say "I want to go there and do this, but..." or "I think I want..." Or, as I hear in my ski shop when I send someone off in their newly purchased gear with the wish that they have a good time skiing, "I'll try." I always wonder how a person "tries" to have a good time. Effort, with an inherent possibility of hopelessness, is implied with that word *try* — the opposite of the ease of a good time. Maybe they should sit by the fireplace instead. But they might have to "try" to sit and receive the warmth also. When customers leave my shop saying, "Have a nice day," I respond, "Thanks, that's my plan." And they laugh. Sometimes it's in appreciation of my optimism, but sometimes I detect a note of mockery at my foolishness in thinking I could plan to experience a nice day. It helps to be single-minded in intent.

Skiers who complain about how tired they are go out for another run. Resort workers hate their jobs and keep showing up year after year. A hotel guest comes into my shop for Rolaids and also grabs two bags of Doritos and a Snickers bar. He sets his mixed drink down on the counter while he searches for money and remarks on how bad his stomach feels. It apparently doesn't occur to him that loading it up with junk food and liquor isn't helping, because he tears into the Doritos as he leaves. You might think it would be wise to keep my opinions to myself, but I feel like an accomplice, as if selling bullets to a gunman threatening to harm himself. So when a customer buys Tylenol "because I'm going out for a big night at the Cowboy Bar," I say cheerfully, "And you're planning on making yourself sick while you're having fun." My husband and business partner, John, claims I belong to the Roseanne Barr school of retailing.

Pure Input

As stated earlier, the body's responses are untainted by anything but actual experience. Yet how often do we disregard this pure input and ignore our sensations or try to talk ourselves out of feeling the way we do? For many of us, this has been a lifetime habit. A relationship with our body, creating a home within ourselves, a friendship in which the mind speaks for the body's experience, is the basis for our relationship with our greater body: the earth.

If we can align all the parts of our being, we are working with, not against, ourselves. Often, we spend an entire day knowing we need to accomplish some task that we just can't act on. I suggest that we ask ourselves why, rather than automatically attacking ourselves for being lazy, irresponsible, or in some other way lacking the proper psychological makeup. Check in with each center — body, emotions, mind — for a response. Often, this involves spiraling through the three areas with our attention more than once, each time gathering further information or stronger affirmation of our first messages.

Chapter Nine

It's a Wild Thing

WRITERS AND JOURNAL KEEPERS complain about not having time to write, but time is a false problem. Behind the supposed issue of time lies a struggle within oneself about some aspect of writing or truth telling. One part of us wants to write; another does not. What if a musical instrument had some of its strings tuned to one chord and other strings tuned to another chord? Darn hard to play music. It's the same with a person. We aren't operating efficiently or honestly if we are not attuned — body, emotions, and mind. In that case, ours is a house divided against itself. If we were 100 percent in favor of writing, we would pick up a pen and do it despite the time factor. Few of us have role models in our lives for writing, so naturally, few of us are completely convinced that we should spend time and energy doing it. When it comes to fueling our systems with photos, we rarely have snapshots of encouragement related to writing to stick into the control center in the basements of our unconscious.

When we fall in love with a man or woman, seldom if ever do we consider how much time it takes from the rest of our life. Writing is like being in love with ourselves and life around us. In all my life, I have only heard one person complain about how much time it took being in love. That was Dorie. "I don't have time to do anything but work, shower, and see David. I really don't like this much." But she didn't break off the love affair, or even consider doing so. Neither should we break off our love affair with writing.

Time is not the problem it seems to be, though I grant that it is as much of an ordeal to manage as money. The problem is those unconscious messages to ourselves that suggest we should be doing something other than writing. My father once told me that if I had spent as much time selling encyclopedias door to door as I had spent writing, I'd be a rich woman. At the time, I hadn't made my first dime writing, and my father figured I must not be any good at it, since in his business money was the gauge of success. Years later, in frustration, I said to him, "I love writing, but maybe somebody should hit me over the head to stop me." Instead of volunteering the weapon as I had expected, he commended me for doing what I loved. With his acceptance of my writing, my father gave me a fine photo to feed into the basement control center. I had been raised in a household that talked about the family business at the dinner table, not art. So like Mitchell, whose story I told in the previous chapter, I was having trouble justifying my time and valuing what I loved. Ultimately, the issue dissolved as I learned more and more to honor my choices.

Try This

Consider your body an altar, a carry-around altar, in the form of breath, senses, muscle, bone, and movement. Wear certain clothes or jewelry designed to remind you of being in the sacred, or present, time and place. In writing, explore how you might do this. Address each of the three centers: body, emotions, mind.

Some of us know anatomy well. Not me. I have purchased a *Gray's Anatomy* coloring book along with a set of painting sticks. I lie in bed at night propped on pillows and color the muscles, veins, joints, and organs of my body. Now when my massage therapist, Olga, works on me, the colors I have chosen to paint the muscles she is massaging pop into my mind. I feel her fingers on my teal-colored trapezius. This area in my body is painful. Olga, a beautiful, lithe Russian, tells me, "You have knot like peach pit here. You much stress."

Consider writing about the areas of your body that give you discomfort. Name the sensations, describe them in as much detail as an anatomy diagram, allow the stories to arise.

Try This

Choose an issue in your life, not something life-and-death important for the first few experiences, but something nagging you today. Become still. Consider the issue in writing; name the parts of the issue. Offer your attention to your body, centering on your abdomen. Attract your awareness with the magnet word *comfort*, and describe in writing any aspect that arises in your consciousness. Ask your body, "What is comfortable right now?" And proceed in stream-of-consciousness writing through the emotion center of the heart and the mental center of the middle forehead, gathering information.

Allow your memories, your hopes and fears to arise. Write down your stories as they come into consciousness. This is a writer's material, original and authentic.

"As far as I can surmise, the mysterious need for narration is seated in the body. What else is a cry of pain or pleasure but a small story?" says Susan Griffin in her book *What Her Body Thought*.

The Link

The urge to create is a wild thing. Creative people need nature, a relationship with wildness. The link between the creative mind and nature is the body. Being true to our energy leads us to harmony with the life forces of the natural world. In other words, this knowledge of our own sphere of energy — the management of our own small earth — leads to joining the universal rhythms of creation. Once writers gain awareness of their bodies, they have prepared themselves for a partnership with nature. This partnership supplies a sense of connectedness to all of life, offers support, and enhances creative energy.

When we, as individual creators, align ourselves with the universal creative forces, the partnership is a powerful source and is an accompanying energy force that shares our passion for self-realization and growth, beauty and order. We befriend our bodies in order that nature can befriend us. Then we are comforted by her bounty, exhilarated by her beauty, fed by her abundance, and energized by her rhythms.

CHAPTER TEN

The Nature of Writing

AS A CHILD, WHENEVER IT RAINED, I begged my mother to let me go out and play in it. I tipped back my head and caught raindrops on my tongue; I splashed barefoot in warm puddles and walked, kicking high, in the flooded street gutters, water up to my ankles. Then I became an adult and ran from raindrops, cringing, to the nearest shelter before my hair got ruined and the press was dampened out of my clothing. What happened?

Along the way from childhood to adulthood, many of us lost our connection to the earth in our striving to become a part of our culture. Clearly, a split has occurred in the relationship between humans and the natural world. How else to account for the deforestation of entire countries on our planet, extinct animal species, mountains mined to nubbins, ice shelves melting?

As a young girl, I used to sneak away from the yard where my younger brother and I played so that I could wander in the woods for hours on my own. But that memory felt like a story from another life by the time I became a mother. I was so tethered to the house that even when my husband and children drove off to the movies, I could not go for a walk in the woods that surrounded my yard. I felt a deep uneasiness that bordered on stark fear; I had severed myself from the earth that much. In the years that followed, I began to make creative writing and journal keeping a regular part of my life, and something mysterious occurred: I ventured outdoors.

First, I strolled the neighborhood, then the nearby parks. Next I purchased my first pair of hiking boots and headed for the wilderness. My family had moved to Cheyenne, Wyoming, by then. At thirty-four years old, and mother of two sons taller than I, I fell in love with Vedauwoo (pronounced VEE-dow-voo), a place whose name means "earth born" in the Arapaho language. "Earth born" describes perfectly this stunning eruption of raw rock located an hour west of Cheyenne. In Vedauwoo I, too, felt newly born to the earth, struck with wonder at the balancing boulders high atop the mountains, the knotted junipers growing in perpendicular seams of dust, and my own body effortlessly walking up steep slopes, the soles of my boots gripping the porous sandstone like the pads of a cougar. This place understood me; I understood this place. We shared a fierce expression of creative energy, pulled it from the same natural source. I was being re-mothered.

The fear of being alone in the dark woods that kept me housebound during those previous years matched an estrangement from my inner life. It felt good to return.

From that point on, I began to seek ways to live nearer and nearer to the natural world and eventually moved to the Grand Teton Mountains. Still, it was a long, slow process of inching out alone, farther and farther, before I took those hiking boots into the Tetons on twelve-mile forays into hidden glacier lakes to eat lunch alone above the timberline.

For me, writing, then connecting to the natural world, happened with the same synchronic pacing of a newborn first taking breath, then seeking food.

Tuning In

Writers need nature. It grounds those of us who spend so much time with the unseen: thoughts, feelings, images, ideas, passions. Anything that successfully pulls us back into our bodies offers balance. Tibetan monks visited my valley to do a sand-painting ritual; they also sold T-shirts that said, "You spend too much time in your head; spend more time in your heart." Nature helps us do that.

We each have rhythms within us. Breath draws in and presses out, heart beats, blood pulses, eyes blink, muscles clench and relax, over and over, with a rhythm that reflects our thoughts and emotions. By spending time in the natural world, we can more easily sense these bodily rhythms, become conscious of them, and in doing so, we also become conscious of nature's parallel rhythms. Tree boughs dip and sway, wind moves, sun glints off leaves and water, blossoms open and close, roots push down, sprouts push up, spiders weave, birds sing, and bees hum, all to a rhythm that reflects nature's aliveness.

In nature, rhythms throb inside rhythms. Days move into nights, and that rhythm moves within the rhythm of the moon, which moves inside the seasons, which astrologers and astronomers teach us are moving inside rhythms of greater scale. Cycles of the planets sometimes take years to repeat their patterns; some take decades.

It's this rhythm or pulsation of life in its universal form to which our own personal rhythms align. Once, humans truly experienced the earth as mother. Now, many of us live as orphans whose lives are so removed from these rhythms that we don't even acknowledge the actuality of them. A Chinese baby girl left by her mother in an orphanage doorway during the night has been fed by a passing spoon, held by an orphanage worker, every six hours. A year later, this baby girl does not know that she can feed herself with her own hands, whereas mothered one-year-olds put everything they touch to their mouths as a way of relating their bodies to the world around them. At this point, the orphan has been a pair of eyes watching life from a barred crib. And we are not so unlike her as we watch life from a window or, worse, a television or computer screen. We don't know that we can feed ourselves — our spirits, our creative energy — from the natural world. We are unmothered.

Wranglers from the local guest ranches in Jackson Hole have noticed that it takes dudes four days of being on the ranch and away from their busy lives before they spot the blue lupine blooming between their newly purchased cowboy boots. Soon after, they discover their cabins have been sitting in the midst of meadows that blossom like exploded rainbows with reds, yellows, and purples. When I was a child and my father was building his business, he used to vomit the first few days of our family vacation as he released his stress and began to ease into a daily schedule of fishing and swimming at our rented lakeside cottage.

Other vacationers never quite release the mental control they're used to in daily life and run their vacations much as they do their businesses back home. Set alarms, organize daily schedules, follow the news, keep track of the stock market, give orders to family members, rush.

One well-known television newscaster zipped into my shop at Snow King Resort one summer morning, held up a swollen, discolored thumb, and said he was on his way to a white-water float trip on the Snake River and he needed a Band-Aid so he could paddle.

I said, "You can't paddle. Your thumb may be broken."

He said, "It hurts a lot, but I'm in a hurry. Can I buy a Band-Aid?"

I convinced him to stop at one of the instant-care clinics we have for visitors before heading for the river. "There's one right on your way."

He rushed out my door before I finished giving him directions, and ten minutes later my phone rang. He was lost. "Where's that place again?"

I imagine, if this man got to his float trip, he whipped up the water with his oar till it looked like meringue. To him, his thumb was an impediment to his plans, not a valuable body part. And the outdoor adventure was merely one thing on his day's list to check off.

How can we have a relationship with the earth unless we experience embodiment? The body is more than an office space from which we carry on the business of life, yet this is how many of us live in our bodies. We even parcel out maintenance to our doctors and dentists without asking questions, as if subscribing to a maid service. The difference is that the body is an organism living in unison with the universal laws of creation.

When interacting with the universal laws of creation, we are drawing from a renewable source of energy. We align ourselves with the breath of the world.

"I come into the peace of wild things." This line from the poet Wendell Berry speaks to the one relationship with nature that is most common among us. We often consider nature a place in which to find peace. Few of us know that we can also find revitalization within it.

My sister said, "Smell this air, Ti." We were a mile inland from the Atlantic Ocean on the coast of Florida, browsing a flea market. Gayle inhaled a big breath and said, "The breeze is coming from the east, straight off the tips of ocean waves, not a smokestack in the path for thousands of miles."

It's this sort of awareness that secures our umbilical cord to earth. I hear those words from my sister, and I am fed an invisible vitamin. The flea market tents and piped music fade, and I am a daughter of the earth. I am reminded of what truly matters: my aliveness here, now. With such intensive awareness, would I litter by dropping wastepaper on the ground? Or light up a cigarette? Or do anything to smother that life pulsating between me and the earth?

No, because I would have to numb out to my senses and to my experiences of connection and aliveness in order to harm my body or my greater body, the earth.

Nature Highs

It might take a bolt of lightning across the sky, followed by a resounding boom, to grab our attention, but when nature does succeed in drawing our awareness, we are pulled out of our egos and into our bodies. We look, listen, smell, taste, and touch. Our senses attach us to the earth, and for this moment, we become exquisitely conscious of a unity with life. In this state of fullness, we experience a marriage with nature. Our bodies are interlaced with the natural world. We are part of the earthweave.

When we are woven into the fabric of this aliveness, the world looks more beautiful to us. Smoothness envelops our being, and contentment wraps us in its fleece blanket.

As we move our awareness from our bodies to nature, we might remind ourselves that digestion begins with the senses. The senses spur appetite for food: the colors of ripened fruit, the scent of fresh herbs, the sizzle of grilled vegetables, the shapes and textures of beans and grains, the sweetness of juice. Food comes from the earth.

Many of us experience a wonderful calming when we take our bodies on a stroll through the neighborhood or lop the heads off spent petunias, stack firewood, water the lawn. Adults often relax by reverting to the comforts of childhood — cuddling in a favorite blanket, sucking on a water bottle, rolling ice cream on the tongue. When life becomes especially difficult, try regressing to earlier historical forms of human behavior: hunting and gathering. Go into the forest and pick berries, gather pinecones or dried weeds for a creative arrangement, track deer. Take off your shoes and socks, and walk barefoot on the earth to soothe yourself further. This moves us to another kind of time, the kind kept not by clocks but rather by the rhythms of the slow-growing things around us, the dip and sway of breeze-blown tree boughs, the pace of nest builders, the easy float of clouds.

Even though we may have experienced nature highs, we don't always honor them for the healing attributes they contain. We often refuse the invitation to give in to them. We may be touched by the grape and apricot shades of a sunset, pause a moment, even comment to another about its beauty; but rarely do we just stop what we are doing and give ourselves over to the experience until the colors gray out. We've lost touch with a kind of vitamin that is available to us in the natural world.

The vitamin comes in the form of an energy state. Energy is the force of being-ness, of which there exist various states. When we are in nature, the shift from one energy state to another often occurs by way of the senses as our attention is diverted from our regular mental activity to the natural world and is arrested there. We halt. We open to the natural surroundings. Our energy moves from perhaps a state of contraction, in which our thoughts were wrapped tightly within ourselves and our concerns, to an expansion of increased awareness. From here, unless we are fearful of a looming danger in our environment, we may soften into a state of diffusion.

Diffusion is the same energy state we experience when we fall in love.

We open our personal boundaries to accept the other; we increase our sensitivities, feel empathy. It's that sense of being one with the world. An exchange of energy occurs with the natural world itself and feels similar to an exchange of intense eye contact with our beloved. A sense of lively awareness extends from ourselves out into the natural world, and a complete acceptance of self and nature follows, with a lack of desire to alter a thing. This blurring of the physical boundaries uplifts emotions and spirit and offers a sense of belonging and ease.

Imagine the flow of writing this state invites.

In nature, we can release our self-consciousness; our public persona or ego has no purpose here. No judgments loom about how we look, act, or feel. The privacy allows sensitivity to our surroundings and ourselves, and as the relationship deepens, we spread our energy wider — up above us to the treetops, down into the duff and root systems of growing things, past tree trunks and undergrowth before us and behind us. We are fully present in place and time. We are enriched through and through. What vitamin on the market does more?

Vitamin of Light

Nature highs are often triggered by light. Near the end of winter, cottonwood trees along Flat Creek send bare yellow branches like slender torches into the blue sky, and in the wetlands, the willows are thick with scarlet wands. Before the leaves come on, these branches are smooth and shiny and reflect the sunlight as they dip and wave in the wind. Their inner throb of aliveness glows so brightly that it seems possible I could read by them once night falls.

Stand beneath any tree, become infused by its colored light, and something mystical happens: we feel the unity between ourselves and all living things.

While I was cross-country skiing this winter at the base of the Tetons, I paused a moment to listen to the silence. I stuck my ski poles in the snow and leaned on them. The winter wind stirred the snowflakes that had mounded on the branches of the pines and lifted them into a glittering halo against the sky as the sun sparked off them. Watching this, I had the sense that I was constructing a vessel within myself that was allowing me to absorb more and more beauty and aliveness.

Perhaps this is our job in life.

Try This

Today, read the weather using all your senses. Record what you see, smell, feel, and hear. Check your body for any responses — for example, old breaks in bones that ache from the cold or dampness in the air, or a kind of excitement in the belly from detecting a change in the season. Predict the weather for the rest of the day. Write it down. This is a good way to deepen our relationship with the outdoors.

To enhance the relationship between your body and the earth, draw an outline of the human form on a piece of paper and color in nature images and symbols on the body. For example: nests, leaves, vines, cascades, flowers, birds, pathways, mountains, stars, rainbows, canyons, clouds, feathers. Decorate it as if the body image were an altar. Tribal villages in Africa are designed to represent the body in some cases. The place where decisions are made is located at the head; food preparation centers are located where the stomach lies; sacred rituals are held in the area of the human heart.

Perhaps one day I will fulfill my dream of a garden laid out in the shape of a body as a daily reminder of my connection with the natural world.

A Life of Relatedness

In our desire to live a life of relatedness to our body and the earth, we may consider using daytime events to inform us in the same way many of us use nighttime dreams. It's a common practice to analyze dream images for insight into our waking lives, so why not do the same with waking images we encounter during real events? Of course, people did this many centuries ago, but we call that "superstition" and tend to think we have advanced beyond that now, with our scientific understanding of how the world works. But perhaps we threw out the baby with the bathwater when we gave up superstition for science, because we also tended to dismiss our relationship with the natural world altogether and the lessons it teaches.

An essay writer, Lone, recognized that her battle with an invasive morning glory in her garden resembled her relationship with her "equally invasive mother-in-law": a battle of maintaining boundaries. She symbolized the lesson she learned from nature by giving the morning glory to her mother-in-law.

My desktop computer crashed earlier this morning, and I called Brett, my computer master, for help. While waiting for him, I felt weak and shaky and kept putting my hand to my chest and taking big breaths as I sat writing outside on my deck. Occasionally, burnt pine needles dropped from above, carried on the wind from a forest fire across the valley in the Snake River range. Brett arrived, checked out my computer, and reported that I had run down its battery by unplugging it from its power source too long.

I caught some of the burnt pine needles on my open palm and thought about my life lately. Burned out? Battery run down? Usually, at this time of year, the tourists in my shop get my worst side. I look at them as if to say, "Can't you people find someplace else to shop?" Also, my writing project at the moment was a book proposal; my muscles tensed from head to toe as I tried to convince an unknown editor that I had exciting material. But I wasn't feeling too excited about it myself.

Had I become unplugged from my own power source? It felt that way. I was arcing my energy and attention outside myself by trying to imagine how to invigorate the interest of an anonymous reader in a faraway place. How about if I directed my attention inward instead and contacted my honest feelings about this project?

I tried the experiment; soon a delicate surge of energy infused me, and the core idea of the project presented itself, reminding me why I had become engaged in the idea in the first place.

Brett returned with a new battery, burnt pine needles continued to fall from the sky, and I wondered if burnouts might do as much good for humans as they do for forests. One of the incident commanders for the forest fire stated in the *Jackson Hole News* that "Smokey the Bear has done too good a job" by telling people that all fire is bad. "This fire," he said, "is probably really healthy for the ecosystem."

In a lodgepole pine forest such as the one burning, new growth only occurs after a fire. It takes the high temperatures of a forest fire to release the seeds from the pinecones. The hot air currents keep the seeds aloft, above the flames, until the fire passes, at which time the seeds float down to a cleared floor that is enriched for new growth.

If this analogy carries over to a human's life, then perhaps some of us drive ourselves to a high pitch before new life, in the form of ideas, energy for change, or calmed emotions, sprouts forth. I have talked to several cancer patients who have surprised me by stating that cancer was one of the best things that happened to them. The lessons they learned about life and their place in it were worth the agony and fear they experienced. Cancer in the body sounds like a forest fire in the wilderness in such cases.

Most of us have experienced relationships that flamed into a rage, then resumed with an improved life in the clearing that resulted. But I would hope we'd all learn to tune in to ourselves more carefully and avoid the need for high-blazing events.

If we pay attention, we can pick up small clues that indicate an imbalance in our lives. My friend Kirsten realizes she has overbooked her life when she begins to blow off appointments and meetings. She's a writer and thinks of this forgetfulness in computer terms as "self-deleting."

Try This

We create a relationship with nature the same way we create a relationship with a person. We spend time in their presence. We offer our attention. We enjoy an exchange.

When working indoors, step outside several times a day and, using your senses, check the conditions. One way to frame your experience is to engage your interest with a few questions for each of the four elements. Include information from all your senses.

Air. What sounds do you hear the breeze carrying? Which direction is the wind coming from? Has the direction changed since you last checked? Do you detect any scents in the air, or feel moisture or dryness on your skin?

Earth. Is the earth frozen, wet, or dry? What's blooming? Touch or taste a stone, twig, or blade of grass. Become aware of the support the earth offers your body; feel your feet on the ground, and pull your awareness up through your legs and spine, and out the crown of your head.

Fire. Where is the sun or moon? How does its placement in the sky change with the time and season? Follow its path across the sky by marking it against the horizon, using a certain rooftop, tree, or hill as a point of reference. Keep track of the phases of the moon; there are charts designed for this, and calendars often supply this information.

Water. Is there moisture cupped in leaves or beaded as dew? Do you feel it in the air or see it in the clouds? Engage your sense of smell in your search for water. Forecast the weather. Step back inside, and offer your body a drink of water; taste it, and accept the refreshment with a conscious moment that connects you to your place on earth and in the cycle of seasons.

Four elements. Five senses. This experience of conscious awareness requires only minutes yet enhances our life with a sense of timelessness.

CHAPTER ELEVEN

Creativity and the Four Elements

OUR BODIES ARE OUR LINK TO THE EARTH. Our senses are our power lines.

Once we create a relationship with the natural world, how can that relationship directly help our writing?

Ralph Metzner says in his wonderful book *Green Psychology: Transforming Our Relationship to the Earth*, "The human being, the planet Earth, and the cosmos are modeled on each other: they *co-respond*." He offers elemental examples of this correspondence between our planet and our body: the winds of the earth match the breath of the body; three-fourths of our body is water, and three-fourths of the earth's surface is water; fire is expressed from the earth as volcanoes and lightning, and in our body as the energy that produces body heat, activates the nervous system, and symbolizes passion.

Metzner discovered in his psychotherapy work that tuning in to the different elements of nature produces an experience of consciousness that is associated with the qualities of each element that is addressed.

For writers, this is a valuable insight. To translate Metzner's findings into a tool for writing, we can offer our attention to each of the elements in order to trigger the associated creative energy for our work.

Air

We can open to the air and align our body rhythms to the wind or breezes, breathing deeply if the winds are strong, quietly if the breezes are soft. We can follow cloud movement across the sky, offering our full attention to the birds, butterflies, flying bugs, airborne seeds, all that is the realm of air. This realm symbolizes change; it addresses the mental plane, involves thought and communication — in fact, writing itself. This is the rational as well as fantastical realm. As writers, we may be especially comfortable here. We enjoy soaring through the skies of our imaginations, darting quickly from thought to thought. Our energy pace may shift easily and swiftly. Often, our perspective can swoop from one side of an issue to the other — as the crow flies — taking shortcuts, without following traditional pathways or landing to connect the dots to new ideas. We "wing it" — take flight with images and words without much notice or physical experience to back us up.

We can offer our awareness to the air element when we need these qualities in our writing: lightness, humor, spirituality, change. And the element of air works well for fast lists, witty dialogue, and overviews.

To experience this realm now, direct your attention to the sky and all winged creatures that pass near. Place yourself in an imaginary wind stream and write stream of consciousness for a few minutes. Experiment with solving a writing problem using the qualities of air that are most helpful to your need:

- Looking for patterns in plot or character? Get some distance on the problem with a "bird's-eye view."
- Need to lighten a heavy scene? Give it some lift while in the outdoors attuned to the element of air.
- Does the pace plod? Quicken the winds of your writing.
- Need surprise? Offer a sudden shift in direction that follows the dive of an osprey, which involves a brief, almost imperceptible halt before the abrupt change. Storms are often preceded by abrupt wind shifts.

Like astrological charts that have most of the planets in the air signs of Gemini, Libra, and Aquarius, characters can carry a preponderance of the air element's traits. They may be flighty, have their head in the clouds, be starry-eyed, put forth a light, easy manner. Imagery from this element can be a useful way to convey temperament.

Metaphors or similes that include air elements — such as feathers, mist, the colors blue and gray, verbs such as *flutter*, *wisp*, and *perch* — can all intensify our writing by using language that keeps echoing our intention.

Earth

The element of earth is considered the practical realm. Its astrological signs are Taurus, Virgo, and Capricorn. Phrases that describe this area are common to us: *down-to-earth*, *rock solid*, *grounded*. This element creates a mood almost opposite that of air's. This is the element to which we offer our attention when we feel our writing is disembodied, too abstract, without meat and bones. Here we can touch the earth, tune in to our senses, and bring the sensory information down into our bodies and produce solid language that is grounded in the physical.

When our writing needs foundation, when a character needs to be strong willed and physically attuned to the scene, we go outside and sit on the ground and become conscious of how each thing — including ourselves — is rooted to the earth. We become aware that this is the source of sustenance for the trees around us and the animals passing nearby. The plants, insects, and rocks, too, all rise out of the earth. These smells and textures and sounds need to be found in our language.

Characters acquire patience here, feel their muscles, experience pleasure. The earth element is a slow-growing, stable, and textured place, full of material for the senses. The images are of mountains and valleys, forests, jungles, deserts, four-legged animals, snakes, insects, rocks, wood. And most especially our own human body.

The element of earth is helpful when we consider

- Plot, building the solid structure of our story
- Characters who display slow-moving, stuck, immovable, or stubborn qualities, or who are rooted in history or culture
- Conveying simple, basic moods, or the qualities of long-suffering, generosity, attachment, fear, or envy
- The simple, basic components of life — food, shelter, mates, heritage, religion (versus spirituality, which is found more in the air or water element), family, organizational structure

Fire

The element of fire is the realm of energy, that often-unseen activator of our actions. In nature, fire is expressed by sunshine, lightning, and magnetic or electrical fields that emanate from the earth — for example, the ley lines that draw people to create shrines in certain areas of the planet no matter the religion of the century. Ireland is full of shrines that currently are considered holy places for Mary, mother of Jesus, but once were shrines to the goddess Bridget and before that, to the earth energy itself that emanated from the spot. The element of fire is often impulsive, or seems to be, as when heat lightning surprises us on a summer night when we are unaware of the unseen conditions from which it arises. Or as happens in human relations, when rage breaks into expression without our awareness of the underlying conditions that created it, as with the Columbine High School killings.

We notice fire itself immediately. It excites us. In our writing, when we want to set the scene for conflict, anger, or passion, we may have someone light a cigarette or a candle or fondle a gun. To create tension, we may use the fire element emotionally as well as environmentally to underline the mood, foreshadow a plot, or define a character.

The astrological signs of fire are Aries, Leo, and Sagittarius. These may be witty people, fast thinkers, large egos, blazing personalities, leaders. Charisma is a fire quality. This is the realm of fiery temperaments, inspiration, addiction, exaltation, smoldering grudges, flaming anger, entertainment, enlightenment, illumination.

The images are halos, sparks, flames, stars, the hot colors of red and yellow, flushes, flares. The fire element is known especially by sound: gunshot, thunderclaps, shouts, drums, explosions.

The element of fire is helpful when writing about

- Flashy personalities
- Abrupt resolution in story or character
- Mounting tension, disaster, conflict, or passion

Due to the fire element's most common quality of sudden, flamboyant drama, the use of it in writing is carefully directed, used sparingly, and often kept behind the scenes as inspiration to fuel the work and as illumination to clarify.

Creative energy itself is a fire element.

Water

The element of water can douse fire, or it can be churned into its own peak images of crashing waterfalls, stormy seas, beating rain, and hail. Water carries the symbolism of emotion, ranging from sorrow to joy, from dark mists to rainbows, from tears to moist lips. It is the realm of sensitivity and spirituality, and its images are oceans, creeks, pools, fountains, fogs, snows, mirages. Water is a strong image due to its importance to life. We have many metaphors in our language that use water's ability to change meaning and effect. For example, to indicate trouble, we say a person is in "hot water," and to douse an idea or plan, we throw "cold water" on it. Water supports life, but in variable terms: if it's too deep, you are in trouble, and if it's too low, you are stranded. Water images create mood and movement with flow or flood, rain or mist, wave or stillness. We use the element of water in its many manifestations to align ourselves with the quality that best suits our writing needs at the time. Water holds the ability to mirror mood in our creative work.

Wally Lamb, the author of *I Know This Much Is True*, told me that he often takes a break during his writing to walk near a creek, which seems to clear his mind and mood. I understood his experience completely since I use water myself to cleanse my creative energy. In the morning, I start my day writing in my pajamas. When I hit a difficult spot, I stop to take a long shower, and I can feel my energy smoothed and clarified. Under the drumming spray, I'll often solve writing problems. In the afternoons, I walk alongside Flat Creek. Scientists explain that moving water balances the ions in our energy systems, which soothes us. I receive its benefits whether hosing my garden or walking the beach; I am calmed and energized all at once in a refreshingly wonderful way.

Astrologically, the water signs are Cancer, Scorpio, and Pisces. These are signs that imply movement, spiritual affinity, mystery, depth of experience, and power.

Try aligning with the element of water in these ways:

- Use the water element to mirror or reflect on character and story line.
- Movement of water ranges from seeping to surging, dripping to flowing. Use an awareness of water's vast spectrum and methods of influence to amplify your creative choices.
- Remember that water is the element of mood. Emotion involves water in our bodies — tears, saliva, phlegm, gall, sweat, blood — and can be reached through nature's expression of water.

- The element of water holds the strongest patterns for rhythm. Consider tides, waves, ripples, raindrops when facing problems of pace and movement in writing.

Metzner also uses the "shadow side of each element" with his psychotherapy participants, recognizing that along with supporting life, each element also represents the ability to destroy, frighten, impede, threaten, kill, or injure in ways that match its energy fields. This shadow side, too, is helpful for writers to be aware of when creating fictional characters and settings. For journal writers, this concept can offer entrance into a greater understanding of our personal lives and situations.

When we use symbols of the natural world, we are using a language that is meaningful to us all, no matter our culture. It carries an archetypal and universal resonance.

Chapter Twelve

Lessons from the Natural World

THE OUTDOORS IS A NATURAL TEACHER for us as we design and conduct our creative lives. Two-thirds of the American people live where they cannot see the Milky Way, according to a report on NPR. So for some of us, nature is an overused patch of grass in the school yard or neighborhood park. If so, adopt it and care for it. Learn from it. Create near it. Wild space is a nest high atop an office tower, shrubbery lining the driveway, a box of petunias, an anthill beside the sidewalk. And always there is the sky, the wind, the earth beneath our feet, even if it is covered in asphalt.

Some people have trouble believing in the value of wilderness — land unused by humans for housing or industry. It's difficult for some to imagine the enlivening effect of space surrounding us and how this space nourishes our spirits, eases our minds, and relaxes our bodies. Many city dwellers accustom themselves to tiny work spaces and crowded streetcars and live contentedly without trips to the beach or mountains. So far, there is no measure of the psychic effect on people who never experience spacious wildness. But I believe just knowing it exists *somewhere* is healing to humans, even if we don't visit it. Perhaps that explains the popularity of nature programs on television. We like knowing the Arctic Refuge, for example, thrives as a wild place even if we don't intend to visit Alaska in our lifetime.

Wilderness is gracious space. It is akin to compassion in our dealings with one another. When we are compassionate, we offer space. We say, "That's okay. We can work it out." We say, "You're doing fine" and "I understand." There's a bumper sticker that states, "Grace Happens," and offering extra space is how grace happens both in the natural world and with each other. Preserving our forests and coral beds is how we show compassion, offer gracious space, both physically and psychically, to the planet and its inhabitants.

And enhancing our creative energy is how we offer gracious space to ourselves. We buffer our spirits from the compacted life going on around us. Wilderness and creativity are both wild spaces. They serve as birthing grounds for new energy; limitless horizons mark their boundaries; life thrives and strengthens in a variety of forms in this gracious space and goes forth into the world to make an exchange with commerce and community.

Lessons from the Natural World

Because of this link between wilderness on our planet and creativity within humans, I looked to nature for direct and practical teachings about living and writing — conducting an exchange between my creative energy, my own personal wilderness, and culture — and I found them.

1. *Live and Write Like a Flower Grows*

A flower does not concern itself with how fast or big or colorfully it blooms. It does not compare itself to other flowers as it develops. A flower doesn't try to control the end result of its experience: who sees or uses the blossom or where or why or how.

Creativity has flow and purpose of its own — like the earth has weather systems — and we need to respect that. While writing, our job is to deal with the source — ourselves, our values, our inner life — and the true expression of that source, without regard to the judgments of others.

Anne Lamott suggests in her book *Bird by Bird* that we ought not compare our insides to someone else's outside. Invaluable advice. Useful in every part of life. For example: Often, Maureen berates herself for not writing as much as her friend Annika writes, before she recalls that she has to fit her family and business into her schedule, while Annika is not partnered, has no children and no living parents, and is financially independent. Rebecca feels unsuccessful in her own eyes because the others in her writing group both write and hold down day jobs, while Rebecca is lucky to find energy enough to punch her alarm clock off every morning. She is forgetting that her marriage is not working well these days; that she found drugs in the car after her teenage son used it; that her parents need a nursing home but refuse to move, making her solely responsible for them; that she is also adjusting to a new boss at her office. Rebecca is in an energy crisis yet is comparing her insides to everybody else's outsides and, naturally, is coming up short.

The spiritual teacher Krishnamurti suggests that we drop our urge to live up to certain ideals and just live with what is.

Ideals pull us into comparisons, fault finding, and stress as we try to measure up.

2. Hatch Only the Number of Eggs You Can Nurture

The robin nesting in my pine tree, called Slash because she has a dramatic slash of white feathers low on her breast, teaches a few things about nurturing that we can adopt for our writing projects. Using eggs as an analogy for ideas often has negative connotations, as in saying a comedian just "laid an egg" when she tells a flat joke. Yet I rather like that suggestion of the possibility of laying a bad egg. We need to lessen our fear of writing down bad ideas in order to relax enough to capture the good ones.

Most birds lay between two and six eggs; that's a good range of writing ideas to incubate at a time. We can learn by watching Slash that not all of her eggs make it to maturity: some young birds fall out of the nest; some die of malnutrition; some become prey. This happens with our ideas as well.

Jot down ideas for writing projects, put each one in a folder, and allow the ideas to become magnets for related material. Over time, as we consider each idea, other thoughts occur around it, and we can write those down and drop them into the folder. We may eavesdrop — or as my niece MacKenzie used to say, "ears drop" — picking up dialogue that pertains to our project or read a news report or learn a fact that is related to one of our topics. Jot down those notes as well and put them in the appropriate folder. Those ideas that continue to engender interest and passion will gather enough material in the folder for us to begin a writing project. Just to mix the metaphors here: this gathering of material can be thought of as feathering the nest because we are beginning to feel at home with the project.

This is a wonderful way to work. The process pulls in the support of other forces around our lives if it is a true subject for us. If it doesn't attract enough material, we let that idea fall out of the nest or become prey, meaning parts of the material gathered may be absorbed into other writing projects. If we have several of these folders, two or three may get all the nutrition from us, as happens when the strong hatchlings in Slash's nest grab all the worms. These are the strong ideas, the ideas we want most to foster; they draw our interest and arouse our passion. Also, due to the gathering material, these ideas start to feel more and more comfortable to us. This meets all the criteria for offering our full attention to a project. Comfort, passion, and interest mean our body feels at ease with this work, our emotions are aroused, and our mind is engaged. This first part of a writing project can feel as if we are receiving support and guidance from the flow of life around us — not working alone, but rather partnering with the offerings of the universe that come our way.

Next take such a folder and begin organizing the material within it. Further ideas will arise as we type the jottings we have collected into our computer, in part because the pressure is off since we already have our core idea and support material.

Finally, rewrite and edit, then rewrite and edit again. For many writers, this process involves letting the project rest until some time passes to allow us to detach from the work. We can read the piece in a different location than the place we originally wrote it, to further the sense of detachment and fresh perspective. Also, we may share our work with a writing group for critiquing, then do another rewrite after considering their input. Power is gathering around this writing project. Though confidence may waver during any part of the process, we have invested enough interest and passion in this baby bird to see it safely fly out of the nest on its own wings.

An important part of the process is to finish our work to the best of our ability and release it.

One of the biggest fears for writers is facing the Big White Empty. Rarely will we fear beginnings if we have prepared for the big, white empty page with the help of the natural events and synchronicities of life flowing around us, using the magnet of our attention. With this nesting method, all parts of the writing process energize the writer to discover what feathered thing will develop.

3. Exult in Each of the Seasons

If the earth had only one season, creative energy would not exist. If it were always summer, imagine how soon the planet would exhaust itself. Yet we often don't feel good about ourselves unless, like the earth in summer, we are producing, accomplishing, achieving. Our culture doesn't honor the times of rest and restoration in a person's life, which is the earth's autumn and winter seasons, as much as it does the productive periods. But we must have these periods for growing deep roots and restoring energy, in order to sustain flow. Over and over again, I hear my writer friends worry about the times in their lives in which they are not producing essays, poems, or novels. One woman bemoaned the lack of work she was doing after the birth of her third child. The winter, when she was usually most productive, was spent enraptured with her newborn, and now summer was coming, when typically she was too busy with her other two children, who'd be home from school, to get any time to write. If only she could have seen four years into the future, when her prize-winning book of poetry would be published, every poem a celebration of birth and nurturing new life. Another friend worried about how much he was hiking and biking and how little he was writing, when he had just completed three years of solid work on his first novel. The guy was exhausted; you could tell that just looking at him. He needed to be outdoors restoring himself and receiving new energy.

Honor the dark and silent seasons. Like the poet's baby, creative seeds root in darkness, begin in silence, and move toward expression.

4. Develop the Balance of Trees

Grow a root system that balances the spread of limbs. Writers need to develop a connection to earth, a relationship with themselves, and a sense of the divine. In short, writers need an inner life, one that matches the outer growth of accomplishment. People who branch out too far without a root system topple from fear or from extravagance. Think of the stories of writers who found success early or easily and those who became addicted to drugs, drink, or fame because of the enormity of their public life as a writer.

My friend Frances had been a senior editor at a major national magazine for several years and then quit in order to write a memoir. Seven months passed, and Frances read, biked, surfed — but didn't write a word. When she phoned me, she said she felt shame over that. Shame. I reminded Frances that trees grow a root system that matches the breadth of their branches. As far out from the tree trunk as you see limbs on a tree is how much unseen growth occurs belowground. The tree needs this for balance and sustenance. I reminded Frances of how many years she had spent branching out in her career as an editor and that her lack of interest in writing now was her inner wisdom allowing her root system to catch up. Frances could trust the truth of these words because all around her on the Pacific coast of the Northwest, she was surrounded by trees engaged in the process of this lesson.

Over and over, nature shows us the rules of creativity. And one of the major rules is that writers need long, deep periods of stillness and awareness in order to express themselves in language that captures the pulsing truth.

I know a writer who produces a novel a year. Sydney claims that she requires only six weeks each fall to write her next novel. According to her, this is also all the time she needs each year to replenish her creative juices. The rest of the time, Sydney travels all over the country, and sometimes out of it, to promote her books. When I see her, it's usually just after her yearly cross-country tour for her newest release, and she invariably stumbles into the airport, looking ragged, with bloodshot eyes and dull skin tones, sniffing and sneezing into a Kleenex. She recovers well, though. By that evening's public talk and book signing, she sparkles up there onstage. But I wonder every time I say good-bye to her how her health will hold up for the coming year.

She isn't the only writer who seems to thrive on a full public life. Along with publishing forty books, Norman Mailer was a political activist and public personality known for his flamboyant ego. A story in *The Writer's Home Companion* recounts that William F. Buckley was so confident of Norman Mailer's strong ego that, instead of signing his greeting to him on the flyleaf of his latest book, which he was giving to Mailer, Buckley turned to the index and next to Mailer's name, he wrote "Hi."

Other writers have isolated themselves from public life; Salinger, for example, when he was living, concealed his identity even from his neighbors. Others have stopped writing altogether out of fear of failing to meet the expectations of their audience. This isolation can also be the result of growing too much inwardly, directing all our attention to our inner life, our roots. A writer who grows more roots than leafing branches is prone to either a souring arrogance or its opposite, a sense of inferiority.

Writing is solitary work; it's tempting to give in to the imbalance of its demands. But as a tree nourishes itself by releasing its leaves to replenish the earth around it, nourish yourself by both replenishing your inner life with solitary activities that deepen your awareness and releasing your skills to your community. There are more ways to do this than publishing your work. You might consider volunteering in local literacy programs, offering to write promos or news blurbs, joining book clubs and writing groups, attending open-mike readings. In this way, we reseed ourselves and work with the rhythm of the seasons, taking in and giving out.

Roots need to grow in the dark for blossoms to bloom in the light.

5. *Howl Like a Wolf*

Celebrate yourself, join your voice with the others in your pack, and let those not of your species know of your presence. Too many of us writers do not speak out, or perhaps even have a history of not challenging the norm with our own original perspective.

We may be people pleasers.

Many of us experience physical problems associated with the fifth chakra, the throat area and energy center for self-expression. Often, we carry stress in the muscles of the neck area and upper shoulders. In our culture, men and women are taught not to voice unpopular opinions. But we are writers because we are stirred toward expression; therefore, we must communicate, possibly for our own well-being.

Writers and artists perform the duties that a wise woman or medicine man does in aboriginal societies. It is our job to be "first aware," to interpret, make connections, detect patterns, and notify the others. We bring into consciousness and put into words what otherwise may remain in the unspoken unconscious of ourselves and our community. Just as it is the job of shamans in native cultures to announce the larger patterns — the weather, the movement of the herds that feed the tribe — we as writers are the ones assigned to be most awake. This is our contribution. We notice and alert the people to ideas, feelings, movements, and changes that are in the transpersonal consciousness. It is as if we are the speakers for Carl Jung's collective unconscious or Rupert Sheldrake's morphic field. We pay attention, we watch and listen and discover the underlying patterns and archetypal symbols in nature, society, and individual growth. Then we speak. We may be a lone wolf out there howling on the ridgetop, or we may draw the howls of other wolves in the vicinity and become part of a group voice. Either way, we must listen, then speak.

Our awareness casts light for ourselves and others to find the way.

As writers, we offer to serve as witnesses for others. By putting words and labels to the pain and joy of living, we provide handles to help people deal with the events in their lives and give them meaning. When we write a novel about suffering through the death of a parent with cancer, for example, we address issues of life that each person in some way experiences — if not the death of a parent through cancer, then the loss of a loved one through Alzheimer's, accident, old age. We must tell our truths because we are mirroring our readers back to themselves, as if we were good therapeutic counselors. Both the writer and the reader are offered healing through this process.

6. Hunt Like a Cougar

Lie low and let life come to you as often as you go out seeking it. This is the other half of hunting. It's listening as often as we talk. It's stopping once in a while and seeing what comes our way. Some of us discover that we are often rushing about doing things, taking care of others, controlling situations, thinking ahead, participating in relationships in which we take on the responsibilities for both sides, ourselves and the other. Stop, rest in the shadow of the sagebrush, and take note of what comes by.

This is interesting to do once in a while with relationships, too. Pause your activities and see who calls you, who checks on you, and who doesn't. I don't mean this in a controlling way or as a needy, passive-aggressive cry for attention. I mean that sometimes we just give, give, give and don't know ourselves any other way or allow our partners in relationships to act in any other way than in response to our actions.

In other words, doing the opposite from what you usually do offers a way of experiencing life anew and of becoming aware of what, up till now, may have been a subconscious codependency or a need to control situations or relationships. There is a time for hunting and a time for lying low; experience life both ways. And your writing and self-knowledge both will benefit from it.

7. Like a Spider, Make Yourself at Home Anywhere You Happen to Be

My house is constructed of logs; spiders love this. Mostly, I leave them alone, but when one weaves a web densely around the top of my lamp shade so that it glistens and glitters in the lamplight, I can't ignore it for long. So I gently capture the spider and carry it outside to the woodpile, where it just begins to spin a new web. Spiders seem to feel at home anywhere.

As proof of this, I read that two female spiders were transplanted to Skylab 3 to test their behavior during the mission. Both spun silk and constructed webs while orbiting the earth.

Spin your web of awareness and capture the essence of place. This means to open yourself to wherever you are and use your senses to capture information, pull it within, and allow it to trigger responses from you. Interact with place and claim it as your own, and you will experience a relationship with it. This widens our vision and deepens our awareness and sense of connectedness, which spawns intimate and authentic writing.

I have moved twenty-three times in my life, beginning as a child when my father was moving up in his field, and into adult life as my husband and I moved to new places in search of home. Never in all those places did I plant tulip bulbs in the fall, though I longed to, because I wasn't certain that I'd still be living there in the spring when they blossomed. How I wish now that I had planted them anyway. I feel regret over my hesitancy to connect to each place I lived, no matter how briefly, because I feared wrenching myself away might be painful. But now I see that I could have acquired instead a sense of home comfort no matter where I lived in the world.

8. Open Yourself to Unusual Alliances
Like the Raven and the Wolf

Ravens are often reported aiding the wolves in their hunt for elk in Yellowstone. After flying over an area, the ravens will call a wolf pack's attention to the direction the elk herds are moving. Once the wolves bring down an elk and finish feeding, the ravens get their turn at the carcass, so the partnership works for both species. I have watched a raven and wolf rest companionably beside each other for over an hour, the bird within inches of the wolf's snout.

In both your writing and daily living, be receptive to the new and different. Talk to people; your interest is flattering to them, and your reward, like pulling a new book off the shelf, will be perspectives that enrich you as a person and a writer. Try new activities and investigate different places. If you always go for coffee at the same café, you might order chai next time at a new spot.

One of the most appealing components to good writing is surprise. If we are willing to invite the new and strange into our lives, we are more likely to incorporate it into our writing. Look for contrasts in setting and opposing qualities in character. Alert writers find them everywhere.

9. Experience the Stillness of Mountains
and the Flow of Rivers

We must be able to hold within ourselves all paradoxes, contradictions, and opposites. This is how we make ourselves big enough to reflect life. Because life is made up of these mysteries, it helps to be easy with the unknown, to hold questions with patience, realizing that no answers may come but that the questions themselves have much to tell us. The important lesson to be learned from mountains and rivers is the unfailing participation in aliveness that each expresses in its own manner. Marion Woodman, author of *Bone*, says that if we cannot hold opposites comfortably in our minds, we will not discover the third way that lifts us above the two contradictions and sets us on our way at a higher level of awareness.

10. *The Sun Beams Its Full Self on the Earth and Holds Nothing Back*

An insight, an idea, a metaphor occurs to us while writing, and we may think to ourselves, "I'll save that for a more important project or an essay that pays more." "Store nothing" is an old spiritual law I found in a tattered book one of my teachers gave me. I didn't understand it at the time. Now I believe it means to shine like the sun, giving your full self at each moment.

We save, usually, out of fear there may be no more where that came from. But as with breathing, it's better not to wait for a good time to do it or hold extra air for later. If we need a good, deep breath, we take it now. We know that with the next breath, the air we need will be available. In writing, we are putting trust in the creative flow every time we enact this law. Write with the full expression of energy and innovation you are experiencing at the moment, and trust that the same flow of creativity will supply you during tomorrow's writing session. Some days are better than others, of course, but to begin saving your original ideas and inspirations is a direct route to drying up altogether.

It's like driving with the brakes on; we are going nowhere fast. Sue Grafton, a mystery novelist, follows this advice and says she never saves a wonderful idea for a future project but uses everything that occurs to her as she writes each book.

Use everything of the moment for the moment.

11. *Snow Falls One Snowflake at a Time; a Forest Grows One Tree at a Time*

The lesson to be learned from this: further the process each day; that's all that is required. Sometimes we don't know what we are writing; we just know we have the urge to write it. Or we know exactly what we're writing, but other forces in our lives prohibit our sinking ourselves into our project full-time. In either case, if we just get up in the morning and require no more of ourselves than to further our process, we will be okay. It's amazing how this small requirement of oneself eases anxiety.

The novelist Sarah Bird says when she gets overwhelmed by a writing project, she lets her stress seep out by taking breaks surfing the internet, shopping at eBay, playing a computer game. Then she goes back to her writing until anxiety mounts again. All the while she is watching her words gather into a manuscript.

I began a huge writing project about which I felt miserably inadequate. I didn't know why I was determined to attempt a thing so outside my realm of knowledge and ability but nevertheless felt that if I were just smart enough — or dumb enough, I couldn't decide which — to go ahead and write this book, it would bring me the wisdom and fulfillment I yearned for. Sometimes I'd have to ask my writing group, "What did I say this book was going to be about?" because I couldn't even grasp the essential idea at times — I floundered that much. I lowered my standards severely one day and said the rules from then on were that I should write down all the stupid things I could think up on the subject of my project. In time, I had a body of work to revise and edit. Later, I realized that, like Sarah Bird, I had created a full manuscript.

I addressed the blank white paper the way a piece of available land creates a forest: one sprout at a time.

12. A Seed Does Not Carry Expectations about Its End Result

Nature goes forth producing a single tree from a single seed and does not profess to be producing a jungle to which the whole world will flock. It grows a tree, then perhaps, if conditions are good, it grows another tree. We as writers have no business dealing in outcomes. We must make decisions from our present state of awareness and reflect that decision in our actions.

How many people read our writing, how they respond to it, how much income or attention our writing brings is not our business — nor is it within our control, and neither should it be. Only the creative process is in our control, and only that process deserves our attention as we're writing.

When we choose a gift for someone, we shop with loving attention, perhaps selecting a favorite book we find inspiring, wrapping it in beautiful paper and ribbon, and sending it off. That has to be the end of it for us. What that person receives may result in something altogether different than what we intended. The recipient may be pleased — or insulted, wondering why you thought they needed inspiration from a book. We need to release our gifts, our seeds, our writing the same way: engage in the process with loving care, then let it go. What the world does with it cannot be our concern.

13. Day Becomes Night, Its Opposite, by Degrees

Everything in nature has its opposite and moves from one pole to the opposite pole by degrees. Night turns into day by degrees; cold moves into heat by degrees. When writing fiction, we are often taking our characters from one position to the opposite position. An unhappy woman becomes a contented woman. A selfish man becomes a generous man. Often, the plot itself is based on this kind of movement. For example, in love stories, two people move from being strangers or perhaps even enemies to being lovers.

As writers, we ourselves are moving by degree from one kind of writer to another, perhaps a novice writer to an accomplished writer, or a tentative writer to a confident writer. The good news is that we can move around anywhere we wish, even from one pole to the other. And we do this by degrees, one step at a time, just as sunrise takes all day to move across the sky and turn into sunset.

14. Wind Produces Great Power but Never Exerts Effort

Although nature in its many forms expresses tremendous might, it never uses effort, and nothing is forced. Nature flows with its own urges and intentions. As writers, we often don't trust our desires, and think we need to force ourselves to write about a certain popular topic for a certain amount of hours each day, feeling righteous over the great effort we exerted on a project. There is a difference between working hard and forcing ourselves to achieve. One invites aliveness, innovation, satis-faction, and flow, while the other compresses our energy into pushing through an obstacle toward a predetermined outcome. Which writing would you choose to read?

15. Everything in Nature Has a Rhythm

All of nature pulses with aliveness, and so should our language. Language follows attention. Beautiful writing looks inward, then outward, inward, outward. Dull pages come from a lack of rhythm. For example, entire long paragraphs of inner musings without any sense of place offer neither movement nor ground-ing. Page after page of description feels disembodied, without human sensation or experience to anchor it. The best work pul-sates with an inner-outer rhythm. In the next chapter, we will discuss further how following this lesson from the natural world enhances both creative writing and the healing aspects of jour-nal writing.

Nature as a Writing Partner

Nature is pure energy, expressed creatively, forever changing. We can partner with the natural world for inspiration, comfort, and nurturing. Living in partnership with nature can also help us produce new ideas and images and draw supporting material to ourselves. This occurs when we open to possibility, honor chance events, become willing to make unusual connections, and experience the outdoors with a willingness to fall in love with essential aliveness.

The energy expressed in this state is one of mellow diffu-sion, vulnerability, curiosity, the same state of energy we may have experienced as a newborn with our mother. We loosen our desire to control in order to allow this way of being to enter us and do its work.

In *The Kybalion*, the law of correspondence says, "As above, so below." Nature is the macrocosm of creative energy, and we are the microcosm. What works on the larger scale, works on the smaller.

CHAPTER THIRTEEN

The Energy of Writing

I BUILT MY HOUSE ON WORDS.

I came home from work one day to the small log cabin to which an addition would be attached. The crew had poured the footers in the foundation of our addition and left for lunch while the cement dried. I recognized a unique chance, found a stick, and carved words into the foundation of my house.

I carved *fun* and *well-being* and *generosity* and *love*. Beneath where my writing studio walls would sit, I carved *flow*, *awareness*, *creativity*, and *exchange*.

Then I went inside the cabin and fixed a sandwich. The doorbell rang, and the crew boss said, "Lady, I am terribly sorry." He looked so remorseful that I looked around for my dog, fearing the crew had accidently encased her in concrete.

He said, "I swear everything was fine when we left...but somebody vandalized our work. Graffiti is scratched all over the footers."

I said, "That was me."

"Ma'am?"

"I did that."

He stared at me, then bellowed over his shoulder to the crew all lined up on the driveway. "She did it." He cocked his head toward me.

Since he and the crew had spent hours smoothing trowels over the footers only to discover the person they did all that for defaced them, I thought I should explain. I said, "I wrote words that were important to me on the footers."

At that, the boss let me know his opinion of my intelligence. He explained slowly, "Well, ma'am... you won't be able to read those words." He paused here so that I'd be sure to get it. "The house will be built on top of them." He seemed to brace himself, as if this bombshell of information would crumple me.

I said, "I know. It's okay; you can go ahead and build the house."

Next he and his men walked all around the foundation sounding out loud to each other the words I had written: "In-spir-a-tion. Clar-i-ty."

I'm a restless sleeper, and I remember now that I wrote *joy* and *vitality* on my side of the bedroom. I might want to change places with my husband, because on his side, I wrote *serenity* and *beauty*, and the sleeping is easier there.

Words are powerful.

The Bridge of Language

We are writers because we are drawn to language, to the music of sound, to story and the power of telling each other things we know. We experience the force of language when we write in our journals. The self grows and glows with the light of our attention. We expand, awaken, and become all we keep looking for in others. Words change us.

For our purpose of creating a relationship between our intimate selves and the natural world, language builds a bridge. It is the connector between mind and body, between ourselves and other forms of energy. Language offers clarity by means of labeling, defining, and sorting, which gives witness to our experience of life.

Our human partners use words as language to communicate and further their intimacy with us, but what language does nature use to uphold its end of the communication with us?

That language may be chance.

Chance

A fellow writer told me a story about something that happened while he was mountain climbing in the Tetons one day. Andy was looking for a new way to the top and found what looked like a natural choice through a vertical stone channel called a chimney. He succeeded in his goal, and when he stuck his head out the top of the chimney, he was met with hundreds of butterflies fluttering around his head. He felt as if he were welcomed by a celebration party. Sometime later, Andy was reading about the American explorer John Charles Fremont's discovery trip to the Grand Tetons and came across an account of Fremont finding this same chimney. And then Andy read that Fremont, too, was greeted at the top with the same experience: butterflies everywhere. Fremont's climb happened 150 years earlier than Andy's climb.

We think of chance as luck, fluke, fate, opportunity, happenstance, serendipity. Accidental events have brought all of us friends, life partners, jobs, and various good and bad experiences. For me, chance has operated all through my writing career as well as through the work itself.

It was a series of chance events, none of them following the usual path of an agent submitting to an editor, that led to my three novels being published by the Penguin Group, and each of those novels is filled with material encountered by chance, too — overheard conversations, light hitting willow wands just right, wild animal sightings.

As a part of raising our awareness, we need to honor chance events. Sometimes we call them mistakes. The poet William Stafford says that mistakes are "disguised reports from a country so real that no one has found it."

In the children's book *Mistakes That Worked*, the author Charlotte Foltz Jones relates that some of the special graces of our lives have come about by chance. Chocolate chip cookies, for example, and tea, Post-it notes, and Velcro were all mistakes. Penicillin was discovered by accident when a mold blew in the window and contaminated a bacteria experiment. Error may be a valid tap on the shoulder from the universal unconscious.

My friend Mary Alice is a weaver and says that her art has won prizes from mistakes. When Mary Alice spots an error, her heart sinks. Then she takes another look and recognizes that abruptly, through error or inadvertent action, she is positioned at a crossroads and has a whole new set of decisions to make. Prior to the mistake, she was moving along directed by a particular pattern and color design with her threads; now she has an opportunity to consider new directions. Mary Alice has learned after many years of weaving to be grateful for these offerings of possibility.

The Ojibwa deliberately place an odd bead in their jewelry to draw off any negativity that may have attached itself to their work from their own thoughts or feelings. They view this deliberate mistake as a release for locked energy.

We must feel this way about our stories. The memories and fantasies that are locked within us and that surface in our consciousness in the third step of a Spirit Walk cannot be dismissed. They arise by chance, triggered by a series of exchanges with nature. They belong to us.

My favorite story of chance, of trusting ourselves and doing whatever occurs to us, belongs to Carl Jung. He contributed so enormously to the study of psychology that I privately think of him as Uncle Carl. The story takes place immediately following his painful separation from Freud, who played the role of mentor, father, and friend in Jung's life. Together, they opened psychological frontiers. Then a point came when Jung could no longer support his mentor's work in good conscience, and they parted. Jung went home to Switzerland and didn't know how to carry on without Freud. He didn't even know what to do when he woke up in the morning. So he decided he would do whatever occurred to him and trust that.

As a child, Jung had enjoyed building small houses from stones. It occurred to him to do that again, and so each day he sat for hours beside the lake near his home, building with small stones and pebbles. Finally, he'd completed an entire village, and in the process, the core of his life's work became clear to him.

Jung said in *Memories, Dreams, Reflections*, "The moment was a turning point in my fate." Jung honored chance and synchronicity, recognized mistakes as signposts, and took cues from the natural events that occurred around him at the moment. For his final project while building his small stone village, Jung needed an altar for the church. He was searching the shore of the lake "with the question of how I could approach this task" when he discovered the perfect red stone; it was shaped like a pyramid. "It was a fragment of stone which had been polished into this shape by the action of the water — a pure product of chance. I knew at once: this was the altar!"

In this story, clues emerge about how to approach nature for aid in living a deeply attentive, engaged life. First, Jung opened himself to interacting with the outdoors and honored his memories. Despite feeling foolish, he then played at a small boy's fantasy as if it were a serious task, going forward with an open mind with whatever occurred to him. When he needed something, he formed the question and then seemed to give it over to nature and chance, while keeping alert for his answer. In this case, Jung found both his perfect stone and the path of his life's work from the country of chance.

William Stafford says, "What a wilderness out there! What splendid stories flicker among those shadows! You could wander forever."

This is the description of a Spirit Walk.

Chance is a wonderful force in our lives. Yet how chance works is a mystery to us. Mihaly Csikszentmihalyi, the author of *Creativity* and *Flow*, states that the definition of chance events is "favorable convergences in time and place open to a brief window of opportunity for the person who, having the proper qualifications, happens to be in the right place and right time."

So chance involves the convergence of three parts: the right time, the right place, and the right person. We usually don't have control over the first two — time and place — but we can learn to be more often the right person, thereby giving chance a more open invitation to enter and create a favorable event. As writers, this helps us at every level of our creative process.

So how can we be the right person for chance to find?

I break the process down into three ways of being in the world: receptive, intentional, and actively engaged:

Receptive. Being receptive means enjoying an open, curious relationship with the world around us. One in which we set aside opinions, expectations, even hopes and, as much as possible, fears. Invite a sense of wonder. Pay attention. Be ready for surprises. Michael Chabon, the Pulitzer Prize–winning novelist, calls this getting caught up in "the slipstream" of writing. He described it in an interview in *Poets & Writers Magazine* like this: "You get into a state where, even when you're not writing, everything you see, read, hear, every place you go; every newspaper you pick up; every conversation you chance to overhear feeds the work."

Intentional. To be intentional is to have a goal in mind that is firm enough to guide us in the right direction, without being so rigid that we miss opportunities. At first, it may appear that this is contradictory to being receptive. And it's true; we need to create a balance to be both receptive *and* intentional. Doing so demands mental and emotional agility. We want to be focused in order not to fall prey to distraction. Yet we also want to remain loose enough to incorporate any serendipitous happenings that arise.

Actively engaged. We have dreams. Perhaps your dream is to become a better writer, a published writer, a writer

who entertains or inform others, or a writer who comforts others. Dreams are vital. Dreams are the fire of
our mental and emotional life. But those flames die
out and become ash in no time unless we take *action* on
them. We must be *actively engaged* in pursuing dreams.
And we must make this engagement an exchange with
life around us.

It's like breathing, taking in and giving out.

When we are in our bodies, with an awareness of place and
a sense of connectedness to life around us, we can trust what
occurs to us and honor impulses. This is our very own material.
We give it language for the same reason we put water into a
container: in order to hold it, to use it for our lives. And to offer
it as a gift to others.

Like Jung, William Stafford let the moment and place guide
him. Many years before he died, I traveled with Bill during a
week of his poetry tour in Wyoming. Every morning, he woke
hours before our first class or workshop and wrote. He wrote
about whatever occurred to him, about wherever he found himself on that day. The result was a collection of poems that captured a true Wyoming and the people with whom he interacted.
Stafford lived so well in the immediate moment that he said,
when asked which poem was his favorite, "I would exchange all
that I have written for the next thing." This remark was made
after more than thirty years of publishing poems. He would give
them all up for the next poem, the next event captured in words.

During that week of traveling with Bill, he more than once
made me dip my head in tears at the reverence with which he
discussed language. Language to Stafford seemed of universal divinity, a sacred container of exchange between self and

experience, and self and others. I wanted to join his church. Clearly, the way to do that was to awaken and to honor whatever occurred to me. My attention and my words were the tools.

Each of us experiences our own flow of chance. As people who wish to raise our awareness, we can begin honoring that. Pay attention to what comes your way. It isn't coming anybody else's way — only yours.

CHAPTER FOURTEEN

Rhythms of Language

ALL LIVING THINGS PULSATE WITH ENERGY; so too should our language. Writing that lives and heals and engages us will breathe in and breathe out. When we go into nature and begin a Spirit Walk, our attention moves alternately inward and outward as we first alert ourselves to body and place, then send our senses out to gather information and pull that information inward. Then, again, we send our senses outward to gather more information and again pull it in, each step bringing our bodies and attention to greater consciousness. When we arrive at the third step of the Spirit Walk, we acknowledge the emotions that arise and let the stories come. Throughout the entire Spirit Walk, our attention moves as our breath does, in and out.

If we continue this rhythm while writing our stories, the writing will come alive to us and to the readers with whom we share our work. We will write these stories with the same pulsation that we experience when naming, describing, and interacting during our Spirit Walk. Inward to our body sensations, outward to our surroundings, inward to our emotions, outward to setting, dialogue, and so on. This rhythm gives rise to writing that is satisfying to write and that we love to read.

Here's an excerpt from *The Shipping News* by Annie Proulx that demonstrates beautifully the inner/outer pulsation in writing: "A watery place. And Quoyle feared water, could not swim. Again and again the father had broken his clenched grip and thrown him into pools, brooks, lakes and surf. Quoyle knew the flavor of brack and waterweed." This example by Proulx begins in the outer with "A watery place" and moves within to emotion — Quoyle's fear. Outer activity and places; inner sensations of body and senses.

Another example I like is from Wally Lamb's novel *I Know This Much Is True*:

> I would remodel her pink 1950's-era kitchen, sheetrocking the cracked plaster walls, replacing the creaky cabinets with modern units, and installing a center island with built-in oven and cooktop. I conceived the idea, I think, to show Ma that I loved her best of all. Or that I was the most grateful of the three of us for all she'd endured on our behalf. Or that I was the sorriest that fate had given her first a volatile husband and then a schizophrenic son and then tapped her on the shoulder and handed her the "big C."

This example is almost a story in itself. We get a full image of the kitchen in both its present form and its future form, but before we ever think, "Okay, enough about the kitchen," Wally Lamb moves us inward — new territory, a wilderness, really. He tells us the thoughts and feelings of his character's inner world. This rhythm is kept up throughout the book in varying lengths, but always the writing pulsates inner/outer.

Whether we are writing in our personal journals or with the intention to publish, pulsation — an inward/outward rhythm — keeps both writer and reader engaged and enlivened by the language.

Writers often fall into two camps. One writes paragraph after paragraph of outer description, dazzling scenery depicted in intricate detail. The other camp goes within and explains on and on what the character feels, thinks, remembers, hopes, and dreads. Despite the talent or skill of the writer, both methods drone a reader — and the writer — into numbness. But put the two together into a pulsating inner/outer rhythm, and the pages shimmer with life.

In chapter 12, we discussed living our lives by balancing our root systems with our outer growth of branches, and this lesson follows through into our writing. We are not in a balanced state of being when we write paragraphs of only outward experiences or paragraphs of only inward experiences.

We are after an easy ride here. In William Stafford's words, "following whatever happens to come along in the writing process." We don't want to strong-arm this pulsating rhythm, though, in the beginning, we may practice making what is a natural occurrence more conscious by deliberately moving inward and outward with our attention. We do want to be present in order to ride what comes along and allow it to take us into whatever wilderness it may lead to. Effort and force have no place in this process. Openness without judgment or expectations for outcome works best. Take what you get, and go with it. Trust your inner authority, as discussed in chapter 3. This kind of writing plants us in the flow of life. "Somehow the language that comes to you when you are truly available to immediate experience can bring you surprises, can enrich experience, can reveal profound connections between the self and the exciting wilderness of emerging time," Stafford says in *Crossing Unmarked Snow*.

It may be tempting, when we first do a Spirit Walk, to dismiss the stories that occur to us. But what if archaeologists reburied their discoveries because they didn't meet their expectations? We would call this behavior small-minded, even unethical. Writers, too, need to brush off the mud from their discoveries and accept them as the rough treasures they are; these artifacts offer information about our buried, less conscious lives.

Try This

Write a paragraph with a deliberate in/out rhythm of attention. Begin with place. Write a sentence describing the room in which you sit or the natural world surrounding you. Follow this with a couple of lines that express inner mood, body sensation, emotions, or thoughts. Then repeat.

This is to practice becoming conscious of the natural inner/outer pulsating attention we engage in normally and to become aware of writing in a rhythm that reflects the aliveness around us and our engagement with it.

Next take a page from your journal or a manuscript you have written in the past, and rearrange your material to reflect a natural pulsation. This may mean that several sentences are engaged in outer or inner awareness punctuated by a single phrase of its opposite. There are no rules to follow about how to do this. The idea is merely to create contrast and rhythm and to mirror the natural attention of humans. Even when we talk to each other eye to eye about intimate, intense matters, our attention flickers outward to the scenery around us and inward to the emotional responses in our bodies. If alone in a dark room sobbing with a broken heart, we would still be aware of someone walking past the door. If awed by beautiful scenery, we would still be aware of an insect bite.

———

Wild Words Heal

In therapeutic counseling sessions, the inward/outward attention to personal detail and outer event while relating our story keeps the experience in balance and in proportion to actual life and aids in the healing process. Often, a counselor asks for outer details and descriptions when a client is locked into her own emotions and not moving through her process. And in the reverse, the counselor requests acknowledgment of personal feelings and memories when a client is frozen into everyone's experience but her own.

James W. Pennebaker, PhD, reports in his book *Opening Up* that he and his graduate student Sandra Beall conducted experiments asking three groups to write about a traumatic event. The first group was assigned to write down their emotions in detail while also describing in detail a traumatic event. A second group was asked to report only the event of the trauma, no emotions. And a third control group was requested to only vent emotions. Pennebaker and Beall requested each group to write for fifteen minutes a day for four consecutive days, then measured their health. The results of writing about one's emotional experience in detail along with describing the outer traumatic events proved in each case to have a dramatic healing effect on the participant's body, with measured health benefits lasting approximately six weeks.

In six months, the participants who wrote about both inner emotions and outer events made 50 percent fewer visits to a health center for illness, while the other groups made more. Pennebaker reports that writers experienced negative feelings in the hour or so immediately following their writing about the trauma and its emotions, but mood, outlook, and physical well-being improved considerably thereafter. Most writers reported a sense of relief and happiness. Pennebaker states that writers who wrote about their "deepest thoughts and feelings surrounding traumatic experiences evidenced heightened immune function." The experiment was expanded to help people endure the loss of their jobs and to heal relationships.

Try This

Recall an upsetting event in your life — it need not be traumatic — and write continuously for fifteen minutes about the event, including physical details and the emotions and thoughts surrounding it. Do this for four consecutive days. Use this method periodically as a clearing exercise for the unconscious. The unattended, unexamined emotional events of our lives drain energy.

Witnessing

Writers give witness. To suffer alone without human acknowledgment is a special hell of its own. It is the fear of prisoners, torture victims, and the sick and injured. Jean Shinoda Bolen uses the term "vision carriers," which applies to anyone writing and witnessing for others.

I have given readings of a short story that came from my experiences with my mother when she was suffering from Alzheimer's disease, and people have approached me afterward to express relief that I put words to the humor, sadness, and puzzlement of caring for an Alzheimer's victim. While I witnessed for them, the listeners witnessed for me. In fact, the short story arose from journal entries in which I was witnessing for myself, translating into words the trouble my mother and I suffered together, which cleared the way for us to better manage the situation. Healing energy was at work throughout each part of the process, from journal entry to public reading.

Writing is a full-circle experience of healing.

A Give-and-Take with Nature

For an intimate relationship with the earth, you don't have to know the natural environment in the manner of a biologist or geologist. You just have to know it in the *manner of you*. Your experience will bring you amazing intimacies and knowledge not commonly known. For instance, select a single snowflake, watch its journey, and discover that snow does not always fall downward from sky to earth, as is commonly assumed, but rather travels in swags like a warbler, darts abruptly like a dragonfly, or actually floats upward for a ways. A single snowflake often does all three before landing.

As we watch that single snowflake, we align ourselves with the creative aliveness of the natural world. When we draw from this energy to write, we make an exchange with nature. Our natural surroundings then create us as we create our art.

The poet Pattiann Rogers calls this *reciprocal creation*. In her poem "Dream of the Marsh Wren: Reciprocal Creation," she tells us how the wren creates the sun through its experience of the sun in the marsh as "blanched and barred by the diagonal juttings of the weeds." And how the marsh creates the wren, "makes sense of the complexities of sticks / and rushes." The wren "makes slashes and complicated / lines of his own in mid-air above the marsh by his flight."

What Pattiann Rogers says in her poem is exactly our goal in writing wild. It is the recognition that we know ourselves through our natural surroundings; that this is the basis for our understanding of all life; and that our natural surroundings create the patterns in which we view life, like the wren who sees the sun in terms of slashes between reeds and who then darts in flight in the same pattern. Rogers also believes that "the land anywhere, the earth, responds to and encourages and itself takes sustenance from such human bonds." The human bonds I believe Rogers refers to are the love and attention we offer the earth. She is saying that the earth receives nourishment from us just as we receive nourishment from the earth.

When writing wild, we give sustenance to and take it from the earth. First, we still ourselves and open to the rhythms of the natural world around us. We breathe the air deeply into our bodies. Second, we cast our net of awareness, using our senses, and pull in a "sense" of the moment. This moment. There is no other like it. This moment is all we need to live fully. The result is sometimes a quick, sharp memory that rises almost immediately, and we begin writing. Sometimes we go deeper into the life of the earth; we lie still and wait; we walk a distance; and we gather a more and more intimate experience of the natural world around us. We begin to synchronize ourselves with the breezes and birdsong; we enjoy a unison of mood and manner. I think of this time as romance — sometimes moving quickly through the mating dance, sometimes going for the deep intimacy, and always building to a pregnancy of creative energy, giving birth to our writing.

Try This

Take your notebook outside and choose a fallen leaf, a frosted twig, a teaspoonful of dirt, and experience this small piece of nature and yourself interacting with it. Do this by first naming, then describing, then letting memories, ideas, wishes, and concerns stir within you. Whatever occurs to you in the moment, you are to trust, for it is yours and yours alone, inspired within you by your openness to nature in this time and in this place, with each step in accordance with mystery and chance. It is of the moment and of the mood, one playing within the rhythms of the other, back and forth, and then producing a third mystery: a story of one's own. A memory stirs, the body experiences a change, emotions surface into consciousness, and scenes produce themselves in our minds.

What we create then creates us. We are altered by our own awareness and language.

———

CHAPTER FIFTEEN

Imagination to Intuition

LUNA, THE TREE THAT JULIA BUTTERFLY HILL made famous with her sit-in years ago, is a universal symbol of the struggle between the natural world and commerce. A few months after Julia came down from the tree, newspapers reported that someone used a thirty-six-inch saw blade to cut through the base of Luna, severing it halfway. Now Luna is bolted together. Sadly, this makes the tree a more exact symbol of the relationship between nature and commerce. That's the bad news; the good news is that the tree still lives, that we have saved it so far, and people all over the world know this tree.

One fall, I was in retreat at Hedgebrook, a writers' residency on Whidbey Island off the coast of Seattle, with a few other women. We had come from scattered places, and only Kate, from New York City, had never spent time in the woods before. The night of the full moon, we went for a walk after dinner. Kate stopped and pointed her flashlight beam upward. "Now, what kind of tree is that?"

Carolyn said, "A fir."

Frances added, "Douglas fir."

Kate said, "Do they all have first names?"

She was joking, of course, but her newness to the forest allowed her to make this joke and all of us to see a common sight with new eyes — a fir, named Douglas. Maybe Kate had the right idea; maybe we should name all our trees. Then, as with Luna, when someone tries to destroy it, the story will hit the news.

We carry just as conflicted feelings about nature as we do about a race of people versus individuals. Once we know the names of individuals, we are open to forming a relationship with them, and so it's reasonable to believe that this may be true as well for trees, wild animals, rocks. Yet since that's impractical, the better way is to become friendly with the wildness itself, to allow what we don't know or understand to exist without feeling threatened by it.

Because deep inside ourselves resides wildness. And we are longing to become friendly with it. *Longing*. *Wildness*. We resonate to these two words. They describe us. Our longing feels wild. Our wildness longs... for what? Union, acknowledgment, connectedness? What do we wish to connect with? Some of us think it's a lover, a soul mate. Some think it's success, perhaps fame, wealth. These ideas, I believe, are only symbols — even the lover and soul mate — for that with which we really wish to connect: our full selves. Our error lies in searching without for what is found only within. We long for a mating with our own wildness.

Perhaps our original sin is the separation from our wild self. Separating our original being from nature may be where the trouble began. In the Genesis story of Adam and Eve holding fig leaves over their nakedness, our culture has placed an emphasis on the embarrassment of their being discovered without clothes, as if the first story of Judeo-Christian creation were about the fashion industry. What our culture does not address is the embarrassment itself. Embarrassment only occurs once we learn to step outside ourselves — separate our inner and outer selves — and attempt to view ourselves with an outsider's eye. There's the crime: separating from ourselves in order to judge ourselves. We left the primeval forest right then. Our wildness was synonymous with our shame.

As always, the answer lies near the question, the solution near the problem, and in this case, the longing near the wildness. Within. Our job is to step back inside our own bodies and lie down on the wild earth. But our culture distracts us from our longing, and so we don't discover our wildness. We are encouraged instead to watch it on television, or to express it vicariously through the cars we drive, or else to abandon it altogether.

True wildness cannot be tested or formalized or graded or given a pay scale — or even completely understood. Art, ideas, invention, nature, intuition: in every case, wildness is welcomed, engaged with intimately, honored without judgment, and expressed. Never contained.

Vanishing Clouds

One April when I finished a large writing project, my husband and I spent a month in a cottage on Hutchinson Island, off the east coast of Florida, a place I have gone all my life. Later, our two sons, in their early twenties at the time, joined us. I remember a particular day when John, our sons, Toby and Trevor, and

I lay on the beach trying to make clouds disappear. All four of us were successful over and over again. We each had our own method: some of us mentally directed heat to the cloud we chose, some dryness; some held an image of the cloud first dissipating then dissolving. It worked best when we chose small clouds, and we could vanish those in a couple of minutes; larger clouds took more patience.

Something wonderful happens when we successfully interact on an energy level with natural forces like that. Suddenly we get it. We know what it means to experience intimacy with the natural world. We do it through the awareness that we ourselves are energy systems and so, too, is all of creation. More than that, we are created of the same energy and share the ability to make an exchange.

There is some resistance to this acknowledgment that we can make a cloud dissolve. I found within myself almost a fear of such intimacy. If I could contact a place within that was as wild as the clouds above me and interact with the clouds to the degree of changing their condition — and likely my own — then what did this say about me? Like Adam and Eve, I wanted to cover up this place when I stood back from myself and judged it. Yet when I stayed within, following my longing, I felt comforted by my relationship with the wild.

When we vanish clouds, we are using our imagination — our creative energy — to picture the cloud vanishing. We send our intention in the form of energy (our attention) to the cloud, and we interact with it. We do this while honoring both ourselves and the natural world. For example, we would not use our energy to turn the cloud into something destructive; and, though I am happy to pass on the news that this lovely exchange is available to all of us, I don't consider it a parlor trick to perform for others, but rather an incredibly stirring event.

Imagination to Intuition

We may take imagination a step further, to intuition. The link again is our attention. We ask for information about what is unknown to us, in the form of a clear question. In the stillness that follows, we allow ourselves to imagine what the response may be. Images or sensations occur. Often, we stop with the mental, emotional, or spiritual knowledge we receive, but I suggest we trust those responses and take action on them. Because without action, our experience is a sun dog — a reflected image much like a rainbow — a vision that is beautiful but does not produce heat, nurture growth, or bear fruit. When the mental, emotional, and spiritual energies are mated with the physical — put into action — they result in a gathered force, directed power, material outcome. In putting our intuition into action, we are working hand in hand with the natural energies. Imagination is a close cousin, if not a fraternal twin, to intuition.

Vanishing clouds relates to both imagination (I hold an image of the cloud dissolving) and intuition (I foresee the cloud's disappearance).

Intuition may well be the exquisite workings of our sensory awareness, as if each of our five senses had a psychic double. We use our senses in a Spirit Walk to awaken our body and connect it to our setting in steps 1 and 2. By step 3, the process has triggered memories stored in the body and stirred our imagination forward to hopes and dreams. The difference between the use of imagination and the knowledge arriving through intuition is divided by only a thin membrane.

Often, when we get an abrupt flash of insight, our intuition has been working to gather information about a person in our company or in our thoughts by divining sensory input of which we have not yet become conscious. We make sudden, seemingly unlinked connections among the various pieces of data our senses bring to us. We may not know consciously, for example, that our senses have detected a particular smell on someone's breath, which triggers a body response of heaviness in our chest, which translates to our emotional center and alerts us to a memory of wanting to leave this person's company the last time we sensed this series of events. Or perhaps the series of images and sensations revolved around an entirely different person in the past. The result is the flash of insight that we are in the presence of a sour and depressed person, and the desire arises to find escape. All the while, our polite mind may be seeking a plausible excuse not to have our energy drained by this heavy, negative personality. This person has not yet said a word to us, nor have we spoken to him. Yet we experience throughout this series of events the interplay between our senses and our imagination, which results in intuitive knowledge.

Many teachers suggest that we act as if something is true in order to help us reach goals, or even change our attitudes. A football coach drills his players, "You've got the ball; run to the goalpost and score points." The coach does not say, "You've got the ball; run around until someone tackles you." Laura Day, in her book *Practical Intuition*, says that pretending often precedes faith. "Indeed, pretending often generates faith, and, before we know it, we no longer need to pretend." Many teachers of intuition suggest that we "imagine" that our intuitive readings on people or events are true, even though it may not seem to make any sense to us at the time. I don't suppose Jung felt that it made any sense when he began to build his toy houses with pebbles on the lakeshore, yet he followed through on his urge and discovered he was symbolically rebuilding his life, stone by stone.

Pretending or using our imagination opens a door many of us keep only slightly ajar at best. Still, from childhood, we have used this realm of the mental world to trigger the sensual and emotional and spiritual, and we can use it again to carry us into the intuitive. In turn, the intuitive puts us into deeper partnership with the natural world.

Try This

Pretend to vanish a cloud yourself as a firsthand experience of exchanging energy with nature. Discovering that this works with such ease at a distance convinces us of what is already happening in our lives, perhaps without our awareness, up close.

Anyone can do this. Choose a small, wispy cloud for your first attempt. Direct your attention to the cloud and try one or all of the approaches I described above to dissolve it. Often, I will "see" a circle of deep blue directly surrounding the cloud I am interacting with, and this blue absorbs the whiteness of the cloud. Dissolving clouds is an exercise in patience, concentration, the power of thought, the pleasure of interacting with natural forces, the experience of oneness with the world, and connectedness to all living things.

My son Trevor is a pilot and has a relationship with clouds that is more intimate than mine. He looks at them from the ground with an awareness that he's seeing the bottoms of clouds. He understands how they dissolve and how they are built and can spot places on a cloud that he calls "sprouts," in which the conditions are good for the cloud to grow.

After dissolving clouds, you might like to work at building them. Take a likely "sprout" and begin to imagine it towering up or spreading outward.

CHAPTER SIXTEEN

Follow Your Longing

"IN THE ARTS, *things* make a difference," William Stafford says in his book *Crossing Unmarked Snow*. "And touching things makes literature." Stafford is referring here to the things of our lives, objects that hold memories, emotions. Stories can be drawn out of the things we have placed in our presence. As Stafford says, "Writers...need to touch the earth; it is a source of strength to them."

The Stone-as-Mother Exercise

Keeping that in mind, let's experiment with creating a relationship with a stone. We can exchange energy through intimate knowledge of that stone via our senses and by imbuing the stone with our personal stories. First, choose a stone from the ground, a stone that is a "stranger" to you, rather than a stone to which you already have some relationship. Choose one that will fit comfortably in your pocket all day and that appeals to you through its shape, texture, or color, or through the associations that arise when you spot it. For example, I often pocket a stone while out walking. Later, I find it as I undress and realize I chose the stone because it drew my desire to touch its smoothness, or my eye was attracted to its unusual turquoise shade, or I thought its shape resembled a Zuni bison fetish.

Next describe the stone in writing with a quick list, using all five senses. Smell it and you will possibly detect a dusty, dry smell, or perhaps a mineral or petroleum smell, or an earthy, moist smell. Give details about the texture of the stone and the sensations experienced through your fingertips; tell about its shape and weight. Write about the colors you see, the ridges and planes it has, and how the light plays on it. Knock your fingernail against it and scratch the stone beside your ear. Go ahead, taste it.

Once you are finished with that list, enlarge your stone in your imagination to the size of a mountain. Place yourself on it and write what your imagined senses may bring you as you roam the ridgeline of your mountain, or sit on a river-carved slope, or stand on a peak or cliff and feel the sense of height, the dizzying peril of standing close to a drop. Consider the formation of this mountain, the years of elemental shaping by water and wind. How might the mountain look in its interior?

Write for five minutes about your experience with your mountain/stone.

First, in this exchange, we alerted our senses by listing details of our stone. Next we offered a deeper description. And we activated our imaginations by making the stone something it actually isn't — a mountain. Yet the stone is a microcosm of a macrocosm — a small system that mimics a larger system, a stone that mimics a mountain. Last, in this exercise of enlarging our stone to a mountain, we put ourselves into the imaginative picture. This exercise mimics what I see us doing in the larger vision as creative people living within a creative system, the earth.

As an aside, the opposite of this exercise works well. When we are standing before the Tetons, for example, it becomes easy to feel overwhelmed by their immensity and beauty. But being overwhelmed is being numbed or stopped if we don't let the feeling flow through us. The next time you are in the mountains, imagine running your fingertips over the peaks and ridges, the valleys and canyons, as if you were a giant hovering spirit. It works as a wonderful way to interact with expansive views of any kind. At the beach, I often seize up before the vast, blue sparkle of it. If I can get the immensity down to personal proportions in my imagination, then I am able to let the flow of pleasure carry me and move me into an awareness of the sand beneath the arch of my foot, the salty taste of my fingertips; I can see one wave at a time and enjoy the sea air.

The next suggestion may sound unusual, but I have used it for myself and in workshops to guide writers rather quickly to the core of their inner lives: write about your stone as your mother.

If we wish to relate to the natural world, we can find a straight path through our birth mother to our earth mother. Our mothers — their bodies, their emotional lives — fed us as eggs within their wombs. Our mother was our beginning. Her essence directed our growth. The grief she caused us is our deepest wound; the joy she spread is our first field of planting and reaping pleasure. First contact. The embodiment of nature.

Her body our planet earth, her emotions our weather. Let her teach us now through her macrocosm, earth.

In this third step, we are prodding our more intimate places by writing about our physical and emotional beginnings, our source of earth awareness: our mothers.

You have probably noticed that we are engaging in a more directed variation of a Spirit Walk with this stone exercise, first naming what our senses bring us, then describing in greater detail, and finally interacting until our stories arise. This Stone-as-Mother exercise stirs the settled bottom of our unconscious. I feel raw side up when I finish this exercise. I write things I didn't know before but that I recognize are true for me.

This exercise is a variation of one William Stafford experienced in a workshop by Robert Bly, in which Bly asked writers to find three wet things from a lake and relate one of them to their mothers. Stafford writes in *Crossing Unmarked Snow* that, when he attended this workshop, he chose a handful of wet mud with "whiskers of root" from the lake bottom. He wrote, in part: "My mother, soft as mud, couldn't survive if we left. She clung with tendrils as fragile as the fragments of root. When she lifted me, my hands imprinted her yielding face as we nuzzled into those last warm days of summer."

That's a high-end example; that's prose by William Stafford. I follow the rule that I learned directly from Bill himself: lower your standards. (This is a subject we will explore more in chapter 19.) Here, I put the rule into effect to offer a couple of lines of my own writing on the Stone-as-Mother exercise: "My stone is broken off from its other half. I am that other half. My mother and I were whole together...or were we broken together? Half moon, like my crescent stone, growing fuller, remembering darkness."

I recommend doing a minute's body reading in your notebook after finishing the Stone-as-Mother exercise. After the above jotting, I wrote: "I feel cracked open, raw and runny inside my chest. Longing swells my insides. I tear up, feel sad, yet content and calm."

We need a relationship with this part of ourselves. We need to touch it and write from it if we hope to experience our own lives with genuine awareness and if we wish to touch this deep place in our readers. This writing experience, which follows the three steps of a Spirit Walk, creates for us a direct path to our core selves.

Keep your stone with you all day today. Then set it where you write, as a touchstone for future excursions into your honest places. A touchstone is defined as a criterion for the genuineness of something, traditionally the purity of gold. Your stone may serve as a reminder for going after the real thing in your writing. Don't be surprised to discover you feel an eerie bonding with this small piece of the earth; you know this stone, your knowledge aroused caring, and, in turn, the stone you chose has told you something new about your mother and about your intimate beginnings. You may feel gratitude.

Nature Readings

My friend Eve is an artist and lives with an acute alertness to her inner and outer experiences. Once she told me she was tumbling a question around her mind while out hiking alone. At one point, she came to a realization, stopped on the trail, and arrived at her perfect answer. Behind her, a small breeze rustled the dried leaves of a broken aspen branch. Eve said it sounded like applause; it made her laugh, and she took a bow.

Readings of the moment are a playful interaction with the natural world, yet revealing, as is anything in life to which we give our attention. By a reading, I mean a brief listing of the things that attract your attention in your environment. The reading can be done indoors, though I prefer outdoors because of the vitality and constant change of the natural world. When a loved person arrives at your door, you take a reading — consciously or not — on this person's mood, concerns, response at seeing you, and you gather any other clues you can about what may happen next. I am suggesting here that we open a door to our environment and to our inner lives.

A reading has two parts: the list and the interpretation. This example was done indoors, beside a window:

November 30th, Hedgebrook Writing Residency,
Whidbey Island

Four o'clock
Rain on roof
Woodstove ticking
Slight chill
Herb tea
Lamplight
Cold toes, left foot
Cedar branches
Rippling water
Desktop
Contentment

Stomach upset

Peppermint Life Saver

My interpretation: Time is an issue. I write it first
thing, and I even describe the woodstove as "ticking,"
as if time is being marked off even with my source of
heat. Cold toes, like cold feet, suggest I am uneasy
about something, a bit fearful. Left foot belongs to the
yin side of my body, which is controlled by the right
side of the brain. I could read this as concerning feminine versus masculine issues, interior concerns versus
exterior concerns, receiving versus giving, being versus doing. Stomach upset equals stress to me. Yet I feel
warmth coming, healing herbs, Life Saver. My conclu-
sion: shortness of time and more stress about working as
a writer than I guessed I would have during my retreat.
However, the general sense is that all will be well.

That was my immediate interpretation of the moment.
I paused to respond to the reading, retrieved slippers for my
cold toes, then went on to write further that I was clearly feeling like a fraud. A writer's residency stirs up such contradictory responses. I was invited to come to this beautiful place and
given my own fairy-tale cottage to live in, meals prepared by
a talented chef, and time around the clock to write. I jotted in
my notebook, "I will never write enough to meet the worth of
this gift. I have a container of home-baked cookies and a vase
of freshly cut flowers on my desk. A candlelight dinner will be
served in two hours. How could I ever write enough to deserve
this?"

Well, I can't, and that's not even part of the deal. I thought

I'd gotten myself straight about that, but my reading of the moment disclosed that I had not. The good part is that I opened to receive information about my condition, offered my attention, acknowledged by naming and describing, and got nearer to the truth about myself.

I knew just what to do next: get outside, despite the rain. I exchanged my slippers for boots, grabbed a light rain jacket and paper and pen, and went for a walk to find the spirit of this forest island and my own spirit — and to let the two make an exchange. The abrasiveness of carrying the conflicting experiences of feeling like a writer and feeling like an impostor began to ease. In the outdoors, there was space enough to hold it all. The walking offered a rhythm in which to process and, as I ducked out of the rain under the cover of a cedar tree to write, allowed me to capture my experience in order to grow from it. Stories came out of my memory that pointed directly to my difficulty in accepting gifts. Hedgebrook was all about accepting gifts of food, beauty, comfort, solitude, creative space. What a pleasant problem to solve.

Years later, I understood the work that I was doing at Hedgebrook. I didn't see its worth at the time, though now it's clear that this book was being conceived. The deeper levels of understanding, the connection between creative energy and nature, were nurtured there.

Try This

Sit outside or near a window in your home or work place with paper and pen. Clear your mind, calm your emotions, center yourself in your body and place. For a moment, close your eyes, then open them and begin a quick list of everything that catches your attention. Include people and animal sightings, bird sounds, fleeting images, thoughts, feelings, colors, smells, body sensations, ideas, weather. Use all five senses to gather your data. Whatever occurs to you, jot down on your page and date it.

Now do a brief interpretation of this list. Respond in writing to some of the following questions and pursue any trains of thought or emotion that particularly interest you:

What tone does your reading express — negative or positive? What concern has been on your mind lately?

What images on your list may be symbols that hold information for you?

Do you sense an overall mood?

How might this list inform a question you have about your life today?

Don't be surprised by contradictory information; that's life on this planet. There is always a mix of negative and positive, yin and yang; this mix belongs in our search for balance.

The outer world often reflects our inner condition if we open our attention to the possibility.

The Call of Our Longing

When we write from our authentic self, we are in contact with our longing for a brimming-over experience of aliveness and a sense of connectedness with the source of all that pulses. Our longing is as mysterious as the deepest part of the forest, the darkest caves of the ocean floor. Our longing is our wilderness within. The heart of that longing may have drawn each of us to becoming a writer. We yearn to venture into the center of things, to feel them and express them to others, so we begin the expedition of writing wild: we address this longing, and in time, we discover how to lead our readers there.

Joseph Campbell, in *The Power of Myth*, tells us, "People say that what we're all seeking is a meaning for life. I don't think that's what we're really seeking. I think that what we're seeking is an experience of being alive."

When most of us hear these words, we fill with a yearning for a grander version of being alive than what we presently experience. Some of us mistake these feelings for a searing desire to have whiter teeth, greener lawns, smaller hips, larger cars, more insurance, less flatulence. TV ads tell us this will satisfy our longing or make us appear satisfied, and by now, many of us hardly know the difference between how we really feel and how we *look* like we feel. We spend hours a day earning money to make ourselves appear happy, healthy, wealthy, and wise... but then something bubbles up, thickens our throat, opens our chest, and calls out to us.

The author Frank MacEowen says in his book *The Mist-Filled Path*, "The spirit of longing is a universal force." He explains, "If we want to discern the difference between the desires of the ego and the longing of the soul, we can always rest in the knowledge that the longing that calls to us will always facilitate a deepening relationship to our lives, while ego-driven desires only serve to separate us from our potential." In answering the call of our longing, we discover our path into authentic writing.

Community, especially sacred or intimate community in which we can freely express ourselves and be heard, is one of the universal longings with which writers especially resonate. Another is a thirst for place, home, a bond with the natural world, a merging with the energy of earth. This longing to merge with earth energies is a natural partner to community. One supports the other. Through partnering with the natural world, we can become more adept at intimate exchange with our community, which consists of our fellow writers and our readers.

The poet Pattiann Rogers says, "All life — beautiful or reprehensible, dangerous or benign, takes sustenance from the earth, all lips that drink, all throats and bodies and roots that seek water." We, too, as writers take sustenance from the earth. That *is* writing wild.

CHAPTER SEVENTEEN

Wild Instincts

THE REENTRY INTO AWARENESS of the body and reconnection with nature stir an intense interest in animals for many of us. For years, I lived without a strong personal connection to our family pets, but this turned into a craving for a dog that reminded me of being an eight-year-old. Besides being plain good company, Zoe and her predecessors, Taggart and Tess, have helped bridge my physical life with my creative life. Before these creatures came to me, I had trouble getting my hands dirty; I didn't sit on the ground or have a daily relationship with the outdoors. I was writing a lot, living in my head and often feeling a bit unanchored. Somehow, these pups drew me into an awakened connection between my body and the earth while simultaneously bridging the chasm between my creative self and the greater creative energies of nature.

At first, my dogs seemed to act as a container for what I couldn't grasp and hold on my own. All that I knew for sure was that I loved their presence, that sometimes a numinous welling up of sensation enfolded me when we were outside together. I didn't get it for the longest time. My experience was one big salad: me, my pup, the outdoors, writing, and insights shooting through me like fireworks.

As my outings intensified, my whole self began to stir and stretch, like a toddler waking from a long nap, and I began to connect the dots. A story told by Marion Woodman in her book *Conscious Femininity* helped. She was rushing to an appointment with the Jungian analyst E. A. Bennet when she learned that her beloved dog had died. She shoved the knowledge aside so that she could make the most of her meeting. But the session did not go well; and at the end, when Woodman confessed that her longtime pet was gone from her life, Bennet asked her how she could waste an evening chattering when her soul animal had just died, and Bennet wept for Woodman's loss.

That term "soul animal" said it all for me. And when I lost Taggart and Tess and grieved so deeply, this story explained my loss to me, helped me honor their leaving. I believe that otherwise, not clearly understanding the intensity of my relationship with these two pets and what they stood for, I might have been embarrassed over my misery. I understood, too, that I was reliving many losses through the ending of this relationship: certainly the death of my mother, then my father, and the loss, really, of my old self — the person I knew so well and who was now, through these new insights, changing faster than either I or the people around me could cope with.

The gifts those two creatures gave me! I wasn't the best trainer with my first dog, Taggart; her rebellion delighted me too much. Often, she and I walked on the elk refuge in the summer after the herd had left for the high country. The rule was that you must have your dog under vocal control, which I mostly accomplished, but at least once a week, Tag would dart from my side on the dirt road and run full out across the prairie. My heart would swell, my eyes tear, and a wide grin spread across my face as I watched her beautiful body race across the land and leap high over the sagebrush, wind separating her black and white shaggy fur down the middle of her face as she circled back to me. If we had been spotted by a ranger, I would have been fined heavily and deservedly. To this day, I feel a teary bedazzlement at the memory. Still, I became a better trainer with Tess, and now, Zoe and I both have learned to express our wildness without breaking the law.

In her book *The Ravaged Bridegroom*, Marion Woodman says, "[Dogs] are an intuitive bridge between conscious and unconscious....Dogs are invaluable to those who love them, because their love is total and they mirror their master's inner world, a world with which the master may have lost touch. Experiencing the dog's responses, the human being makes the inner connection. They are like us, but other, a step toward the humanization of wild instincts." The words explain my experience perfectly. My dogs, first Tag, then Tess, and now Zoe, are much more than my pets or even my companions; they embody my wild instincts and offer guidance for my soul work. They act as ambassadors, linking my inner life with its outer experience.

We also live with Miko, a long-haired cat, shiny as onyx. Each animal in my house brings its own dimension of wildness to my life, as much as the redtail hawks that ride the thermals above my house, the moose that lunch on crab apples in my garden, and the cougar that slips down the mountain to the creek across the road at night. All the animals I welcome into my life link me to another dimension of my wild instincts.

Animal Selves

Carl Jung states in *Mysterium Coniunctionis* that "it is worth noting that the animal is the symbolic carrier of the self." So our relationship to animals, whether intimate, abusive, companionable, or dissociated, is the acting out of our relationship to our soul, the very seat of our creative energy.

A Wyoming rancher of my acquaintance grazes cattle on the same land his father worked and his grandfather homesteaded, and on which his sons have been raised to do the same. The family's roots are deep in this land. The homesteaded cabin still rests on a mountain slope. Indian tepee circles dot the pastures. But one summer, this rancher knowingly shot the last bear that lived in his county. The rancher saw the bear as a predator around his calves. He buried him on his land, swearing his ranch hands to secrecy. What was the rancher really burying?

Wolves were reintroduced into Yellowstone National Park and by now have roamed into the mountains and forests outside park boundaries and are spotted by ranchers, hikers, and hunters. Some people thrill to the sight and sound of a wolf in the wild; others are angry; others are fearful. Some people believe the reinstatement of the wolf into the wilds represents a move toward valuing feminine energies, which include creativity and the natural world; others see the wolf as a threat to their financial investments and safety.

In *The Unfolding Self*, Ralph Metzner writes that this duality of thought in regard to animals must be brought into harmonious balance, both for the sake of our own health and spiritual well-being and for the preservation of the world of nature. I say this is true regarding our creative selves. This duality of thought must also be brought into harmonious balance, both for the sake of our own health and spiritual well-being and for the preservation of the world of nature.

If we can learn to honor the wildness within, we can value the wildness without.

Often, we treat our own creative energy as if it were a fearsome and fascinating wild animal. We cage it in a certain place and time in our life. We find it unpredictable, capable of making sudden leaps or slithering into hiding and other times capable of camouflaging itself in the background altogether. We feel a lack of oneness with our instinctive and creative selves; we are motherless this way, in that we have few role models. Sometimes, we consider our creative selves just plain scary, like Bigfoot or the yeti; and sometimes, like those two mysterious legends, we don't believe that our creative selves really exist.

The English word *animal* is from the Latin *animale*, meaning "living, animate," and that word comes from *anima*, meaning "soul." In our culture, those seeking soul knowledge and expressing it in creative energy are often treated the same way wild animals are treated: sent to the far edges of the territory, if not actually caged. When funds dwindle in our educational systems, usually the first thing to go is the arts. Yet like animals, artists, too, are seen as a resource. In my community, nonprofit organizations in need of money often request that artists donate their paintings, sculptures, pottery, and jewelry for resale to help fund projects, as if artists can keep producing more and more art as cows produce milk — it's assumed at no cost to them — and therefore don't need reimbursement for their efforts. When art is purchased, it is often displayed to exhibit wealth or status, the way the heads and antlers of wild animals are used as trophies.

Artists and animals are at once expendable and prized. A paradoxical relationship, for sure.

In both cases, the value rises when the animals and artists are dead. Once an animal species nears extinction, its worth as a trophy rises dramatically, and the death of any artist whose work is shown publicly increases the artist's fame and the price of her art.

There is a kind of fear in response to the untamed, whether it's a mind or a creature. Stories or myths become attached and are passed on with both dread and fascination, like the legends of bears and tigers, Hemingway and Fitzgerald. Tell a neighbor when you first move into the neighborhood that you are an artist, and they may become as uneasy as if you'd just announced that your dog is a hybrid wolf. You are viewed as unpredictable and therefore scary, possibly dangerous. The range of unease is wide: you may have AIDS, odd friends, unusual ideas, or merely peculiar lawn decor.

Try This

Recall the last animal you spotted or the first that comes to mind now — bird, insect, four legged. Describe any characteristics you may have in common. Do not disregard any creatures because you prefer not to align yourself with an alley cat or earwig. Accept what occurs to you and write a stream-of-consciousness paragraph or two about this creature. Surprising connections will arise.

Charlie wrote about an ant, grudgingly at first, but then warmed to the subject and realized that he and the ant were related in the way they worked intentionally, walking right over obstacles, without changing pace, to reach goals. He was a good team player at his job, industrious, single-minded, and didn't always know when to stop. Charlie wrote for fifteen minutes about this lowly creature, remembering how he had watched an ant struggle to drag a potato chip across the sidewalk, and joked that he, too, would do almost anything for a potato chip.

Honor Your Ancestors

Animals are linked to humans and to writing, in ways that surprise and comfort us. For example, according to Jim Harrison, author of *The Road Home*, the Chinese ideogram for "writing" is a tiny group of animal tracks.

The connection between humans and animals begins with sound in childhood. Children find fascination with animal sounds and often mimic them as their first expressions of speech. In the beginning, humans learned communication from animals. Birds whistled, elk bugled, owls hooted, whales sang, lions growled, and wolves howled. These sounds designated territories, answered mates, celebrated hunting success, related distress, passed on migration directions. Likely, the first communications of humans imitated these sounds, and the sounds became the labels of people's needs — language.

Many myths and religions, as Ralph Metzner points out in his book *The Unfolding Self*, view creation and evolution as beginning with animals, going on to humans, then gods. That idea means humans, standing midway, carry within themselves characteristics of both animals and gods.

Perhaps wild animals are our baby pictures.

If chance is the language of the natural world, animals are its main messengers. One summer after I had lived in this valley for eleven years and never spotted a single snake, snakes showed up a dozen times while I was out walking my dog along the creek or hiking in the mountains, things I had done every summer in the previous years. Then, just to be sure I got the message, my husband and I were hiking along the Boiling River in Yellowstone and were stopped on the path by two enormous snakes mating in the middle of the trail.

During my summer of the snakes, I was in the midst of huge changes in my inner life and experiencing fast movement from being a dependent homebound wife to becoming an independent writer who was falling in love with the creative process and the natural world. Of course, I didn't know consciously what was occurring at the time. All I knew was that half my time was spent exhilarated over my writing and the self-fulfillment I was finally brave enough to seek; the other half of my time seemed spent in tangling emotionally with every single member of my family, from younger brother to older son and husband, and parents in between.

After being a good girl and people pleaser for over forty years, I began to back off from that role to use my time and energy for my own interests and passions, and the sudden reversal of my ways caused disruption all around. No wonder I thrilled to my dog Tag breaking her training and bounding illegally across the refuge. She was showing me how it was done. Meanwhile, as these changes were playing out, I went walking and encountered snakes. Always benign snakes, and in every case they were crossing my path. After so many encounters, I became perplexed and sought out symbolic meanings of snakes. I found the symbolism ranged from spiritual transformation and healing to snakes being one of the main delusions of insanity, and all those meanings seemed to fit my condition perfectly — most often the last one. Since the majority of people around me were suggesting I just knock it off and return to my old self, it made sense that I might be crazy. Yet it never seemed easier to just discount my experiences and go back to living my life for others. My mother suffered from early-onset Alzheimer's disease and died before she could fulfill all the things she imagined. My choice seemed clear: I had to give this way of living in the world a chance.

Of all the relationship changes occurring in my life that summer, the one with my husband was the most worrisome and the most important to me. Often, I had joked that John and I had been married several times during our three decades together because we had experienced many different relationships with each other, and that summer we lived through a few of our marriages all within a single season. When the mating snakes lay before the two of us on the path, something within me eased. At this point, I began to relax and trust life. I had the inexplicable knowledge that all was well, that all was going to be well, and that the snakes crossing my path were symbols of my own skin changing — an event that, despite the trouble it was causing, was an achievement I had long desired. Now I have lived another eighteen years in this valley — happily, with my marriage intact — and recall only two more sightings of snakes in that time; both sightings occurred when I needed my batteries recharged.

This is exchanging energy with the natural world. It's the process of give-and-take at work on the energy level. The energy of nature restores us. In return, we restore nature when we accept these gifts and follow the natural train of feeling toward any source of gifts: the desire to give back.

There was a time in my life when I could have ignored the snakes crossing my path. Or if I noticed them, I wouldn't have wanted the event to signify change or suggest I might have to respond in any special way. Once, I may not have captured the experiences in writing and connected them to the stories of my life. But, like many writers who say they write in order to know what they think, I also write to pin down what I feel and match it to the circumstances of my life. We are building something here: a deeply aware life. Feelings are fleeting, and we want to get more out of them than someone who is content to allow their fast passage and then numb out. By capturing the events of our lives in words and allowing the natural world to speak to our condition, we live a more intentional life.

Try This

Release your imagination to pretend you are exchanging energy with an animal. A goldfish, a robin, your pet salamander, a deer in binoculars — choose a creature you have access to for several minutes. Offer attention, undistracted, full-bodied. Experience the animal through all the senses available under the circumstances. If you choose a pet dog or cat, give her a massage, following the muscles and bone structure with your touch. Notice the animal's reactions. If you choose a wild creature, do it all hands-off but expect a response.

Through a spotting scope, I have watched a grizzly sow with her three cubs on a mountain so far away she wasn't even a speck on the slope when I looked with my bare eyes, yet she paused in her digging and turned her head over her shoulder to look right back at me. Last week through my glass door, I silently sent admiration to a tiny chipmunk, delighting in his intricate markings and feeling gratitude for having one in my yard for the first time. He pattered straight over to the glass and stared back at me.

Birds at outdoor feeders are a good choice of an animal with which to exchange energy. Instead of viewing as usual, drop a few notches deeper, settle in, and begin to sense the bird's rhythm. Soon you'll capture the sensation of the quick dips of the head, a breeze lifting feathers, the tail flickers. Nothing mystical here. Just the easy next step to bird-watching. And a flexing of your creative ability as you now write about your experience.

Animal Dreams

For many of us, dreams take on a mystical importance. They come in darkness, are surrounded by mystery, and demonstrate depths and widths to our imaginations that impress us with all the unexplored caves and peaks within us. Why not give this same attention to our outer world? Why not read the symbols, ask ourselves the same questions about the beings and events around us, and get our clues to who we are and where we're going? In a dream, if a white butterfly wings past us once, twice, lands near us, and reappears in a later part of our dream, we may take it as a symbol to be acknowledged. We may look up the possible meanings in a dream book. If the same thing occurs in our backyard some afternoon, we are likely to ignore the event. Yet we could be missing a facet of our experience by doing so. Why not pause to notice what we were feeling or pondering during the repeated appearance of an actual white butterfly and reflect on the issue with greater attention?

One night, a friend named Shara dreamed of a moose standing still and looking at her. After a while, Shara noticed that he was missing a back leg and that his antlers had been removed and were used to prop him upright. No more than that to the dream: the moose, hind quarters propped on antlers, staring at her. The dream haunted Shara for weeks. The *Medicine Cards* handbook, conceived by Jamie Sams and David Carson, stated that the moose represented self-esteem. The antlers are a symbol of a moose's power; this moose had his antlers almost out of sight and was using them to rest on. That seemed to describe Shara to herself perfectly. She hid her power — as women of our culture are sometimes taught to do. She pretended not to have any unpopular opinions, disowned her insight, and belittled herself with humor. She couldn't accept compliments graciously and was uncomfortable with success in any form. Shara was sitting on her power. Once she became mindful of the meanings she pulled from the dream, she began to make changes that incorporated this wisdom.

Shara got a lot out of her dream image. And it has stayed with her for several years now. In contrast, a moose occasionally walks into Shara's garden in real life, and she uses the information to wow tourists or impress her family back east. Shouldn't this physical appearance carry just as much information as a dream? Once we begin accepting these gifts from the natural world, our exchange with life operates from a broader foundation of meaning. This skill of awareness gives depth and range to our writing that can't be duplicated by any other means than our own interaction with life around us.

Animals as Guides to the Divine

Animals were the spiritual teachers of our ancestors. From watching animals survive, humans learned how to live on the land. Animals showed the location of water, where to hunt for berries and roots, how to find shelter. Humans admired and emulated certain skills and characteristics of animals: cunning, bravery, patience, observance, nurturance. These qualities were held in honor, valued in the community, and in time, revered. Animals are still very much a part of Native American sacred songs and rituals and the stories that hold their morals, history, and understanding of life.

When I touch the sun-warmed stone beside an ancient petroglyph — a horned mountain sheep, a bison — I am convinced that there is a link between animals and our sense of the divine. These are sacred sites; reverence ushers in an awareness not just of the stone animal drawing but also of its placement — often facing water, a rise of land, migratory trails that travel past, the sky overhead. Animals, earth, the divine. And a deep sense of how it all comes together in a human being surges to consciousness. I capture it in language, and, later when I am home, after the sun goes down, I tug on the fabric of words to pull forward the experience and wrap myself in the weave of life's evolution that was expressed in stone by others hundreds and thousands of years ago.

Animals play spiritual roles in many traditions. As Ralph

Metzner reminds us in *The Unfolding Self*, it is told that Jesus was born in a stable with animals all about him. In Egypt, India, and many other countries, stories and art portray humans residing between animals and the gods and goddesses. Animals, humans, gods — the pattern repeats over and over again. Humans depicted in ancient art with physical animal parts, horns and tails, and godlike auras and halos, performing acts of kindness, healing, praying.

Animals as Mirrors

Carl Jung writes, in *Synchronicity*, of counseling a client who was describing a dream in which she was given a golden scarab, or beetle. At that moment, a beetle flew into Jung's window, which, Jung writes, "contrary to its usual habits had evidently felt an urge to get into a dark room at this particular moment."

Jung accepted the idea of chance happenings, even a series of them, as mirroring an inner state of being and therefore as quite personal in content. He tells a story of encountering fish seven times in various ways — often involving other people — within a two-day period while he was privately studying the symbol's historical meaning. Because the country of chance is a wilderness to us and the mystery of its events is so often symbolized by animals, it is wise to give attention to our relationship with the creatures that share our experience on earth.

By creating a relationship with our own wild animal within, we offer a valuable service to the world on other levels. As above, so below. As within, so without. As we honor our own wildness, we will honor the earth's wildness.

CHAPTER EIGHTEEN

Writing Wild

HOW MUCH DOES our outer world mirror our inner world? I am not promoting a way of life that leans on outer symbols as divination about our inner selves. I do promote living an alert life that accepts comfort, assurance, even guidance into our inner explorations from chance encounters in the outer world.

Living a life that's sensitive to chance events and encounters carries the same benediction for one's happiness and welfare as driving at night: may you stay awake, watch out for wild animals, follow the light.

Then write about it.

Wild Instincts

How does acknowledging our wild instincts directly help our writing?

The Spirit Walk process operates as a form of meditation. Meditation is bringing one's consciousness to an alert, focused awareness, and the benefits are calmness, clarity, and insight.

These qualities translate into a clean, ordered thinking process that directs our writing into clean, ordered prose that uses the moment — chance, language, sensory data — to express itself.

Arnold Mindell, in his book *Working on Yourself Alone*, says, "Meditating on the earth gives you a sense of her inexhaustible generosity and abundance and her truly endless patience. Though environmentalists would argue she is less patient these days...the old earth is still yours, full of power, telling you things no human being could."

Earth is the one constant throughout the history of humankind. Contemporary people think of our planet in terms of humans and cultures; aboriginal people think of the earth as populated by trees and rocks and animals as well as humans, seeing the earth as a force capable of informing and healing — in other words, in terms of energy exchange. We can begin a new relationship with the earth immediately by widening our awareness of the natural world to include this idea.

Mindell suggests an exercise to reconnect with the earth: go outdoors, sit, and lay both palms on the earth.

I would add: be still and, without intellectualizing, become aware of each of your senses. Since the senses connect your body and your consciousness to the earth, you experience original perception at such a moment.

If we can be in relationship with the earth, this "mysterious, messy fountain of energy" as novelist Joy Williams calls it, we become clear in our firm sense that the earth is in relationship with us. The process evolves through awareness, which we approach and strengthen with our writing, which then in turn clarifies and sharpens awareness.

The old traditions of divination may seem a bit spooky to

us in the twenty-first century, but the earth hasn't forgotten the old ways and lends itself to renewing the practices in new ways. Herbal medicine is a wonderful example of this. The study of martial arts and yoga that is so prevalent now also honors the traditional relationship to the earth in their teachings. Many of the positions in yoga, for example, are named after birds and animals. Ceremony has returned; the use of ritual to honor and express distinction and reverence is again common.

The new practices require much more responsibility from the human end of the relationship. They recognize the laws of physics and don't relinquish any personal power or control over life but do open us to appreciating the natural world as a living entity that offers important information to us about our lives.

I am talking again about chance and how, in opening further to its play in the mystery of events, we can gain insights into, and a wider perspective on, our place in the creative systems of life. For instance, Kendrick wrote a novel-length manuscript and turned it in to his agent, who passed it on to readers, who in turn reported back to the agent. The consensus was that Kendrick's novel needed a clarified resolution; the characters needed to come together, if not in peace, then at least in acceptance of one another.

Kendrick took his problem to the woods. It was snowy in February, and wildlife was scant; many bird species had migrated south for the winter, and small mammals were hibernating. Trees bare, creeks frozen, the whole forest seemed to reflect the cold whiteness of his blank computer screen, and Kendrick felt that his three years of work on his novel had drained him of creative ideas. He came to the woods this time not for inspiration but for a solid idea about how to heal his manuscript. With this question in his mind, with the need in his emotions, and with his body willing to lend itself to the rhythms of the natural world around him, he walked at a pace that matched his searching mood and the snowy, crisp forest. He alerted all his senses and consciously listed to himself what he heard, saw, smelled, tasted, and touched. He paused and let himself be attracted to whatever drew his interest or affection: a ragged cloud, a seed husk rolling atop the crusted snow, the call of a chickadee.

Kendrick told me: "For a moment, it all felt connected, separate parts of one whole, tacked onto the present place and time. And I knew that my story also had all the parts that would connect it to one whole, that each character in my novel carried a particular quality that would draw that member back into the resolution of the story. And I also discovered that one of the characters had to trigger this vision of wholeness and hold it for the others, just as I was holding the pieces of this moment while the cloud shifted shape, the seed husk lodged against a tree trunk, and the chickadee flew away. And I knew just which character could do the job."

Some time back, I studied with Frank MacEowen, a shamanist in the old Celtic tradition, whom I quoted earlier. He says that he takes his clients "hillwalking" to find symbols from the earth to give them direction or guidance about the questions and healing needs in their lives. One woman discovered a broken branch that gave her the answer to how she could mend her broken and scattered family. Each day of our class, Frank laid an altar in the center of our circle, placing stones and sticks he found while hillwalking nearby with his questions about how best to guide us during the day.

An important part of this form of divination is to enter the natural world with a questing spirit. If the Lakota had done their vision quests with an attitude of refuting the events around them, denigrating the energy and beauty while disregarding the emotions and thoughts that occurred to them in the midst of these natural places, we probably wouldn't have heard of them and their powerful and colorful culture. Vision quests, shamanic journeying, hillwalking, ceremony, and Spirit Walks all require a seeking mindfulness and an amplified awareness. MacEowen says in *The Mist-Filled Path* that a "flowing intuitive way of sensing that is rather slow in rhythm is best." He adds that "to access the wisdom and healing of nature, you must slow your personal rhythm down to match the soul energy of the spirit of nature."

In the same book, MacEowen says, "I recommend keeping a journal of the images or sensations you encounter in nature in relation to your question. If you treat these images like waking dream images and keep a faithful record, you will slowly discover that you will begin to see with your own unique symbol system."

When outdoors with a questing spirit, I am aware of something else at work. I think of this "something else" as a magnetic field. My creative energy flows with a special grace, my mind moves with acuity, and language arrives as music. A similar thing happens after I attend a lecture or a reading by a writer I admire. I return home and write better for the experience of being in the skilled writer's company. Possibly we all do, and that explains why we attend readings, conferences, and workshops. In the presence of a good writer, we are not consciously thinking, "I've got to use more active verbs." It's more potent than that. We are thinking, "I want to do this. I want to write, and I know that I can." We are full of clarity and inspiration, and the desire to act on them. This is the same thing that can occur in the outdoors. We can spend time in the magnetic field of the natural world and leave feeling cleansed, full of clarity and inspiration and the desire to act on them.

If we remain open to the images, symbols, and sensations that chance brings our way, we refine the guidance of the natural world. In *Green Psychology*, Ralph Metzner says, "Symbolism speaks to the emotional and sensual aspects of mind, not just to the abstract conceptual mind. The language of symbols and images connects our ordinary awareness with the experience of the deep, living, organic, archetypal patterns of nature and cosmos."

So our intent is to look past the externals and see what others miss, and write about that. Writers are not domesticated or tame. They do not see only what everyone else sees, but rather they take the time to look beyond, look closely, amplify, take apart. Writers listen deeply to the chords of sound around them, label the separate ingredients of a fragrance, taste the earth in an apple, touch tree bark, feel breezes on their skin, and become more and more conscious of the response of their emotions to their body sensations. Let us not allow those inner events that cannot be measured and graphed to fall away. We cannot lead a valid writer's life without those immeasurable aspects of aliveness: emotions, thought, insights. This is the realm of writers. This is where we need to be doing our work.

CHAPTER NINETEEN

Care and Feeding of a Writer

WE ALL HAVE FULL LIVES WITH FAMILIES, friends, and work, and we don't wish to shortchange any of them. So the question is how to find a way to meet our personal creative needs while not shirking our relationships and responsibilities. Take into consideration the rote instruction airline attendants give about using the oxygen masks. They tell us to put the mask on ourselves first, then attend to others who may need help. We do nobody any favors by neglecting our own needs. We want the children of the world to see their parents doing what they love, so that they, too, will grow up knowing how to do what they love.

Many of our mothers and fathers were taught to give up their lives for the sake of their mates and children. This sacrifice was necessary, perhaps, for the times, but not what we want to pass on today. When we take our first breath, we take on the job of living our own lives as our first responsibility to the life force of the universe. Doing so consciously is what we want to pass on to the children.

Time, Again

People greet each other with the happy question "Been busy?" and their faces fall in dismay if we answer, "No." It's assumed, in that case, that we've been recently jailed, sick, or just unpopular. It's too easy to be busy these days. The hard thing is to make choices, draw boundary lines, and act on these decisions. Why does our culture treasure being busy and consider it a measure of living a successful life? Why don't we revere silence and stillness, and ask each other, "Been idle?"

We discussed time and the conflict we have with it in chapter 9. Managing time in our practical everyday life is a big issue for all of us. William Stafford said he woke very early every morning — four, five o'clock — and wrote. In *Crossing Unmarked Snow*, Stafford said that when people complained they couldn't find time to write, he had to "avert [his] eyes, not to look accusingly at them." Because he knew that they, like all of us, had the same amount of time that he did and that they, too, could choose to wake hours earlier and use the time for themselves.

From Bill Stafford, I heard, as I've said before, my favorite writing advice: lower your standards. Bill was referring to a way of staying in the flow of creating poems. He recognized that we lock up creative energy with our expectations and with the high standards we borrow from others, and he was recommending that we free ourselves from these standards and allow ourselves to write what he termed "insignificant poems." He wrote consistently every day, Stafford said, by lowering his standards. He just kept lowering them until images came, then words, then connections. For him, it was all about the process, not the product. We can take that message into all areas of our life, reminding ourselves that it's all about the process, the experience, the quality of awareness. We can use those words — *lower your standards* — to liberate our life in every conceivable area, from cooking to Christmas shopping.

That's where the time comes from. We find extra time for raising our awareness through lowering our standards.

Lowering Our Standards

Many of us feel rather proud of how high our standards are. Recently, a neighbor said to me that she yearned to do something creative. "But," she said, with a touch of arrogance, "I'm a perfectionist." Like Stafford, I wanted to avert my eyes, because she may as well have said, "I've paralyzed myself — and I'm proud of it." Because that's what she was doing to herself: immobilizing her creative energy and somehow feeling superior about it. This, of course, is fear disguised as something more comfortable sounding to our ears.

I said to this woman, "Well, the things I do that give me pleasure I do way below perfection — knitting, gardening, jewelry making." I smiled and, using Stafford's words, said, "I have very low standards."

She laughed and said I couldn't possibly mean that. Yet I do, and I gave her an example. I'm soothed by knitting; but I don't like to follow intricate patterns, so I knit square things — scarves, throws. Well, my neighbor said, if she were to learn to knit, she'd want to make fancy sweaters or just forget it. So there she is, and unless she lowers her resistance, she'll be in the same place next year.

Every time we think we must accomplish something or must accomplish it in certain ways, we can consider how we could lower our standards and move on, allowing more time and energy for the things that really matter in our lives. This is the core idea behind the many books out now about simplifying your life.

We can lower our standards about how much money we earn; the car we drive; the clothes we wear; how much yard work, housework, and writing we do. We can even lower our standards about the quality of our writing.

Along the way, I have picked up tips from others on how to lower my standards and clear time. From my sister and sister-in-law, who both own businesses, I learned to dress simply. Gayle and Debbie chose an appropriate outfit for calling on customers and attending meetings, then purchased enough of the same mix-and-match components to just reach into their closets each morning and get ready for the day without hassle. Men have known this trick for years. The idea is to just decide on a uniform, stick with it, and use your creative energy and time for more interesting decisions. All winter, one writer friend wore cords and turtlenecks, and every morning found it amazingly freeing to release the struggle of solving the same old puzzle: What should I wear today?

Housework advice came from Annie Dillard, author of *Pilgrim at Tinker Creek*. In an essay, she wrote, "It's endearing how people think writers have time to dust." We should make a sign saying that and hang it where houseguests will see it. We could leave the last word blank and fill it in to accommodate our current need. "It's endearing how people think writers have time to — vacuum, mow the grass, wash the dishes, cook."

My domestically skilled friends alerted me to the time-saving value of deep freezers. Now when I make stews and soups, bake bread and cookies, I make large amounts and freeze future meals. So when it's my turn to cook and I am deep into my writing in the late afternoon, I just open my freezer and chance frostbite in order to create dinner.

Many of us live in a constant flux of social obligations. Time with friends and family is important, yet, often, we may yearn for unscheduled time alone, daydreaming, writing, walking outdoors. Realize that we may be meeting someone else's standard about how much time we should spend socializing or how often we should phone, visit, set up activities. When we become clear about our own desires and feel comfortable about how much solitude we need in order to write and to enjoy a creative life, we can cut back on our social obligations. Then our time with others is spent without anxiety, because we can be fully present, without half of our attention engaged in an unmet yearning to be alone and write.

An interesting thing happened to my friend Jenna when she dropped the expectations she had about what she "should" do socially. Jenna backed off from tending her alliances for a brief time while she worked out the demands of her life, and in the process she discovered who made an effort to keep up the connection and who didn't. This told her that she was energizing some relationships almost entirely on her own, and with that information, she made a conscious decision about whether to continue doing that or not. Of course, some relationships are necessarily based on one person doing the caretaking; an eighty-year-old parent or two-year-old nephew, for example, may not be capable of visiting or perhaps even phoning, so we do all the work if the exchange nourishes us.

Many things become clear once we sweep clean the time and

space in which to address them. The reason we don't make this time and space in which to clarify issues in our life? Because we prefer to numb out so we don't have to acknowledge the issues, accept their reality, and work to solve them. Often, this process is painful to ourselves and those we care about, but we need to offer our relationships that kind of honesty. It frees up not only our energy but also the energy of the other people involved.

Some people and activities drain us of our passion and interest and comfort; some enrich us. That is just a fact. We tend to be more unaware of the drains we experience, because, as with a slow leak in a tire, it's hard to notice or even to discover just where the leak is located. But we need to deal with these leaks, or else we'll be caught flat, right when we hope to roll.

One of the best things Rick, for instance, did for himself was install extra shelves and hanging space in his closet. "I felt a definite ease in my body, as if some nagging thing stopped pulling on me. The closet is organized, everything visible, easily reached, and even now, a couple years later, I still feel soothed at the sight of its simple order." The French novelist Gustave Flaubert said, "Be regular and orderly in your life — so that you may be wild and original in your work." Sometimes, reaching for order is as simple an act as organizing our sock drawer. Whatever it takes to lessen the chaos around us makes way for clarity and creative energy and frees our attention to the moment. The moment carries our material as fully conscious beings, and we don't want to miss it.

It helps to remember that we don't need to be everything to everybody; we just need to be somebody to ourselves. Lowering our standards, simplifying our lives, gets us there. Yet this is easier said than done. Even Thoreau, perhaps the father of this idea, didn't always follow his own advice. My husband, John, says he wants to make a T-shirt that uses Thoreau's quote "Simplify, simplify, simplify," with a big *X* crossing out two of the repeated words.

Dumping Horses

The horse latitudes, also called the Doldrums, are an area in the ocean that explorers first encountered on their sailing ships while traveling to the Americas. Near the equator, the ships were often becalmed, and time became a race against the shortage of fresh water. Sailors were pressed to dump precious cargo overboard: their horses. Only through such a drastic lightening of their load could the ship move out of the calm and back into the current that would carry the sailors to their destination.

Times occur when this way of thinking is necessary; usually, we consider them emergencies as they involve illness, accident, or a threat of some sort. But sometimes, personal occasions arise when there are no threats to our physical well-being, and yet we are stuck, becalmed, in a slump. When it seems that we are going nowhere fast, when we are occupying the same place in the current of time, circling without flow or growth, and want to move on toward a goal or just back into the stream of life, drastic moves are called for.

When feeling stuck and out of flow, drop everything you can manage doing without. I call it "dumping horses" because we must let go of precious cargo — events and encounters we may consider important to our life. At such times, recognize that we must release these things for the amount of time it takes to center ourselves on our goal or to unburden our time and energy in order to get back into a flowing current of aliveness. Difficult decisions are involved, but it does no one any good for us to die of thirst.

The image of dumping horses seems harsh, yet it depicts the magnitude of the choices we often need to make in our lives. Erin wanted to finish writing a book, yet she was becalmed in the process, with no space in her schedule for the necessary months of solid work. She needed to write this book when she felt it pushing out. "As with the birth of my sons," Erin said, "crossing my legs until a more convenient time occurred for everyone wasn't going to work." She felt frustrated, without wind in her sails. Erin began dumping horses: she canceled her traditional fall camping trip to Montana with her extended family; she backed out of a yoga retreat; she called off breakfast meetings and lunches with friends. "I messed up other people's expectations and plans for me, and I found it daunting to do so," Erin said. "Yet I also discovered that I had the strength and courage to look after myself and knew how to direct my life back into an exhilarating flow."

The Is-ness

Accepting the "is-ness," or reality, and using that as a guideline toward a truer life frees us from the tyranny of our ideals. J. Krishnamurti says in *Freedom from the Known*, "It is a brutal thing to have ideals." He explains, "To live completely, fully, in the moment is to live with what is, the actual, without any sense of condemnation or justification." Often, we don't want to become aware of and acknowledge the is-ness in our lives because we fear we won't be able to stand living the reality of it anymore. And that's true; we won't. We aren't supposed to stand it; we're supposed to know the truth, act accordingly, and move on. Life is meant for flow, for movement. The good news: once we become conscious of the way it really *is*, we have already changed our relationship to it. Numbness — not knowing — is a fear response; so is forgetting. People who plead forgetfulness or ignorance are saying in effect: "Leave me alone; I don't want to be responsible for this knowledge. I want to be allowed to live without that awareness." Accepting "what is" is composed of the topics we have discussed throughout this book: living in the present; connecting with the natural world; awakening to our senses; following our awareness into our bodies; acknowledging our emotions; allowing our stories to rise; releasing outcomes.

The Challenge

When Anna Quindlen, author of the novel *Black and Blue*, is on book tour, people come up to her and say, "I've always wanted to write, too." As if the two of them, Quindlen and her fan yearning to write, have this thing in common. Quindlen says to such people, "Desire is one thing, action is another." You can imagine how slammed you might feel if you were the one approaching her with your longing. But Anna Quindlen is right, even kind, to express this truth. The person hearing her response has two choices: she can feel insulted and decide Quindlen is a rude witch, or she can move her desire into action and possibly into a manuscript.

Consider accepting this challenge: determine that what is important to you will get first priority in your life for the next six months. I'm not recommending that you give up Saturday evening dinner dates with your partner or playing with your kids or walking with your dog or talking with your friends. I *am* recommending that you put a strong emphasis on *yourself*. That you carry out a dream. That in six months from today, you will be saying to yourself, "I did it. I carried out my intention to clear the way and make the quality of my personal experience uppermost in my life." It's a challenge I have accepted myself.

If you yearn to write or write more: begin now.

At the end of the six months, you will have learned about yourself as a creative person in a distracting world. It's amazing how becoming conscious of such a decision changes everything around you. When you put a conscious intent into your life, it both creates a frame that makes a protective boundary for you to work within and draws challenges to your intent.

By the end of six months, you will know what challenges arise, from whom, and from what areas in your life; you will watch yourself crumble in the face of them; and then you will watch yourself stand up to them.

You may learn for the first time to say no. No, I can't do that, go there, volunteer for this, take on more now. I am going to live my life. I am going to write. I am going to see who lives inside me.

Oh, the trouble we can have with the word *no*. We are afraid someone is going to challenge us and say, "Don't you think your child or aging parent or best friend is more important than messing around with your paper and pens?" Or "It's not like you're going to earn a lot of money from it, so what's so important?" On and on. And we don't have good answers to any of those questions. Yet there is only one person in our life who would ever ask such harsh, rude questions. And that's ourselves. Sadly, many of us talk like that to ourselves.

Giving ourselves six months as an experiment in living, as a research project, as a way of furthering our self-knowledge, is something most of us can do.

Here's what Chris said about accepting his six-month challenge: "Though I had been writing for many years, I carried a yearning to write more. I was bottlenecked with my longings. And then I decided to try this experiment. Immediately, my relationship with myself as a creative person altered. I saw my work in a whole new light and respected myself more as a writer. Also, I found an amazing amount of things could be put off for six months."

When you keep lowering your standards, clearing time and energy for your writing, you are likely to reap the extra bonus of realizations that had once eluded you. That's what happened for Suzy. She was surprised to realize that she was expecting herself to uphold her creative life while meeting social obligations every week with friends who were financially supported by their husbands; did not hold full-time jobs; did not engage in creative work of any kind; and were childless. Yet Suzy expected herself to live by their values and schedules rather than her own as a working single mother of two, who wanted very much to write a novel.

Once we get into the routine of making ourselves the first concern, we gain a new perspective on every single part of life. All our relationships — with time, work, play, and people — shift. At the end of your first six-month challenge, you may discover that so many of those things you thought you had to do defined a person you are no longer interested in being.

By now, I have renewed my challenge several times. Each time is a brand-new experience resulting in a fresh view of life in all its aspects.

Something pure occurs when we prioritize our lives in an honest way. We align ourselves with a larger truth, and it works in our favor by energizing us. We may never again have to engage in that struggle of ourselves versus everything else in our life in quite the *undefended* way we were struggling before we took on the challenge.

Statistics show that each time a smoker attempts to quit and fails, it improves their chance of success the next time. So perhaps each time we attempt to begin giving ourselves the position of importance in our own lives that we crave, we strengthen our chances of succeeding.

Shoulds

I once heard a metaphor that describes what happens when we begin to release the "shoulds" in our lives. A boat is moored by several lines on all sides of it so that it rides securely on the waves. Once a couple of lines are cut, the boat bounces around a bit and bangs against the pilings. When more lines are cut, the boat bounces and bangs more. When all the lines but one are cut, the boat is in serious peril of destroying itself during high winds as it crashes against the pilings. But when the final line is severed, the boat floats freely. And it can ride out serious storms safely.

That's us with our list of things we "should" do and be. It's not an easy process to release ourselves from them, but the freedom to ride the waves is worth it.

We can have *so many* demands on our lives. Perfectly decent, justifiable demands. We must put "first things first," as an old spiritual law suggests, and let what we love attract our attention more and more. We must act on our dreams. To dream without action turns us into ungrounded, insubstantial people. To take action without direction from our dreams turns us into gerbils on a wheel. Living truthfully while following our dreams clears a trail for others, showing those behind us how to make a creative life work. It's worth noting that this entire struggle we have with ourselves and with the demands on our time and energy strengthens us to carry out our work.

During my six-month challenge, every time I began to think, "I should do this, I should do that" — shoulding all over myself — I would say, "I'll look at that again after my challenge; for now, I will follow my life."

The Power of Lists

Lists are a wonderful solution to the problems of time and energy management and set the paving stones on the path toward lowering our standards. My sister, Gayle, is married to a writer but hates to write herself. When she feels troubled or life seems to be ganging up on her, her husband, Bob, advises her to make a list of what's on her mind. The objective of such a list is to make ourselves consciously aware of what may be operating at an unconscious level, doing its dirty work in the dark.

Libby operated the activity desk in the same resort where my shop was located, so we often talked between customers. She told me one day that when she got upset, she grabbed paper and pencil and listed words describing her feelings as fast as they came to mind. She discovered that the first stream of words that she wrote were negative and that, if she kept going, the words became more positive. She also used this method of listing when she was trying to understand a relationship. "I just write one word after another, whatever comes to mind. Usually, it is emotions, but sometimes I add colors to my list. Colors are important to me."

After leaving her home state of California and moving to Jackson Hole, Libby felt miserable in her new location. She wrote a list naming all the bad things she could think of about living in Jackson Hole. She missed her family, old friends, the ocean, and the costume shop where she had worked. Then she wrote another list naming the good things about living in Jackson Hole. Libby said, "The good list was a whole lot longer than the bad one." She began adjusting to her new home right then. She found new friends, began skiing and hiking in the mountains, and opened her own costume shop in Jackson Hole.

Libby used this method of listing to help a friend. He was experiencing a difficult time and not feeling very good about himself. Libby said, "I just wrote whatever words flashed into my mind about this man: emotions, colors, characteristics, things, and places. I liked him a lot and just wanted him to know that." She mailed this list to him. "It's surprising the feelings and ideas that come up when you do this," Libby said. Her friend phoned to thank her. He told her that it made a big difference in his life to see himself reflected in the eyes of a person who valued him.

There is always time for a quick list. Or consider an ongoing list that you add to as thoughts and feelings occur around a particular subject throughout the day. A list can heal, clarify, direct, organize, simplify — all with so little energy and time required, yet with big rewards offered. In writing lists about ourselves and experiences, we are tending our lives, becoming alerted to problems and pleasures, naming, describing, and retrieving our stories. We can work on a list while waiting at a stoplight or in comfortable leisure, in solitude or in public. A list is an informal way to keep track of where we are at any given time and a guide to where we wish to head next.

Listing is a natural pattern for our minds. Children love lists; this is how they learn. Many of the first stories heard, such as the Mother Goose rhymes, consist of lists; for example, a list about bags of wool in "Baa, Baa, Black Sheep." When Keeley, age four, and Zander, age three, lived in El Paso, Texas, and traveled by car to my house, they listed the sights from the Rio Grande to what they used to call Grand Ti's Mountains — and other people call the Grand Teton Mountains. A three-day trip consisting of thousands of miles was reduced to a manageable list.

In *The List Poem*, Larry Fagin teaches us how to write poetry using lists. He says, "Lists and catalogs are among the oldest written documents and occur in the literature of most cultures." Consider writing poems from the sensory lists you made about a particular moment in your environment that were suggested in the Try This section in chapter 16.

Listing is a method that aligns with the earth's natural processes of both breaking down into parts, blossom to seeds, and building back up again, seeds to blossoms. A Spirit Walk itself is a listing of lists.

Here is a list of listing ideas:

Things I shouldn't say
Qualities I admire in others

Angers
Gratitudes
Fears
Dislikes
Worries
Wishes
Comforts
Pains
Pleasures
Reprimands heard as a child
Hoped-for changes
Beliefs
Loves
Things I can release

CHAPTER TWENTY

Wild Spirit

BY DOING WHAT WE LOVE — writing — we become more and more awake, moving into our true selves with every word.

There is no adventure more exciting than the search for self and the discovery of one's own source of energy. Both parts — search and discovery — occur through writing our stories, as I have been discussing. By now, we understand that the journey is a spiritual process, based in the body and rooted in nature.

Once I gave writing a prominent place in my life, I changed so much that my family suggested something might be wrong with me. As I mentioned earlier, I had trouble with every relationship in my life, from my two sons to my brother and mother. You have to question your mental stability when you're that much in the minority.

Trouble on the Path

It all began when I read Saint Augustine's words "Love, and do what you like." A revolution quietly occurred in my heart. Then it got noisier. In no time, it involved more and more people. One night, it came to a head at my house. My husband, John, along with our two grown sons, still living at home off and on, turned off the television and came to the dining-room table where I sat. They didn't actually say, "Stop writing; bake cookies." But they did suggest that I was ruining our nice family and that I should change back.

I used to figure that if I could just make my husband and sons happy, then I would be happy. But after twenty-some years of living with other people's priorities guiding my life, I rather abruptly put my own in that position. In my heart, I had wished all three every good thing, but they were on their own as far as fulfilling their dreams. I was picking up the trail of fulfilling my own.

I was writing.

Through the process of doing the creative work I loved, my sense of self was constellating, its seemingly unrelated parts coming together, forming a whole and rising into sparkly consciousness. It was a sudden event, though all my life I knew in a shadowy way, as deep unmet yearnings, these qualities that I was now experiencing as my own. Almost as if I were aching for a lover, another half that would fulfill me, this yearning often disguised itself as a desire to assume a certain appearance, buy something, travel somewhere, meet someone, stand out. I know now that my longing was for my true self in all its fullness, with all its many facets.

When John and my sons approached me that night with kind smiles to suggest that I stop my craziness, I eventually realized they were prompted by fear and were responding to the abruptness of my change. Maybe they actually missed the cookies, but I know that even more, they missed me. Still, at first, I couldn't see their fear; I was engulfed in my own.

I spent the night sitting up in my studio, asking myself, "Am I crazy?" Proving the possibility to myself, I sobbed out of control.

In the hours just before light, I knew the truth, or as much of it as I could handle right then: never in my life had I felt so happy or alive as I had in the past few years; if this was insanity, I was sticking with it. I napped a bit, then went to the woods, hiked to Bear Paw Lake, cried more, got stronger. Later, I spoke with my husband and sons. After living with a smiling hand servant for twenty years, my guys could use some help adjusting. And so could the smiling hand servant. Though I understood something about what was occurring, the ripples from it were in danger of drowning the lot of us.

Because suddenly I was quite angry. Even furious.

The question that haunted me was: Why did those people who loved me so well let me sacrifice my life for them?

The answer, it turned out, was because I insisted on it. I would have it no other way. You couldn't have stopped me with the Tenth Mountain Division. I was full-out bent on resisting my own life and the responsibility of living it. I believed full-heartedly at the time that the highest potential of my life was to make everyone else's life happier. Even I could see how those who dearly loved me experienced some resistance to my breaking away from that devoted path. More than homemade cookies was involved.

I will never forget that night, the sudden shock of realizing who I had become and knowing there was no going back. My husband and sons were supported in their dissatisfactions by the abrasions I had also created with other family members. If this had come down to a vote, it would have been one against many.

Fortunately, that's not the way my family works. When love is involved, everybody needs to win.

It took years of patience and forbearance on all sides. Anger, arrogance, and other dark emotions that didn't fit my sunny helper-to-mankind countenance now bounded out of the shadows and performed gymnastics for any audience that could stand it. And the surprises weren't all about me. As in many other families, alcoholism was a problem, and in the case of my mother, it was disguising the even larger problem of early-onset Alzheimer's disease.

I learned that once we become strong enough to acknowledge our true selves, we see the true selves of others. And that begets its own challenges. We may discover that we've consigned our best qualities to overlay the actual characteristics of family members and friends. And when we reclaim these qualities, recognizing them as our own, it leaves others a bit naked, perhaps not as attractive as they used to be while dressed in our projected disguises.

All of us in my family worked out our difficulties because we all cared enough about each other to invest the energy to do that. My relationship with every one of them is more honest and loving since I'm operating from my authentic self. Sadly, that person isn't much of a cookie baker, but it turns out that my husband and sons are. Seems that once we get honest with ourselves and live from that, it clears the space for others to do the same.

Switchbacks All the Way

I don't mean to scare anyone off from this wonderful adventure with my admission of the trouble it may cause ourselves and others. It is worth it, and the process itself prepares us for the outcome.

We cannot ignore our urge to create. To do so deadens us. We can only proceed with our lives while ignoring our creativity if we numb ourselves. These sense organs of ours, our eyes, our ears, our nose, our tongue, our skin, and their psychic doubles, become alert in a creative person and bring us our truth; they need to be exercised. If ignored, these senses fade to the unconscious once again, and so we die a little each time we make a choice not to act on our yearnings.

Jim Harrison says in *The Road Home*: "Art is at the core of our most intimate being and a part of the nature of things as surely as a tree, a lake, a cloud. When we ignore it, even as spectators, we deaden ourselves in this brief transit."

Creative living in action is a love affair with the essence of yourself and thereby with the essence of aliveness. You beget and multiply and give birth. Pain is involved, and unimaginable joy and fullness. Disappointment is a part of this process; so is failure.

But what is it, we must ask ourselves, that wishes to hide or stop trying, that feels embarrassment, perhaps even shame, at this perceived failure? For some of us, it is our ego, our outer sense of ourselves. We wish to protect our self-image, keep it looking successful. Some of us put a halt to our dreams when they come up against the dreams of those around us; it's just too darn hard to stand up for ourselves. Some of us stop our progress toward self-knowledge and self-expression because the process unearths agony, injury, and malice, and the pain is more than we can bear. Some of us are ambushed by fiercer beasts on this path than are others.

At such times, we need to slow the process without halting it altogether. The path to self-awareness through creative expression, with support from the natural world, is a gentle path that can be walked by each of us at our own pace. We can slow the process by offering a hand to those on the path behind us; we can proceed once again by asking for a hand from those ahead of us.

We must face the grief in our lives if we are to become honest writers. Without that journey through our bodies and emotions, our memories and fears, we cannot write deeply enough to touch others in ways that lead them through their own lives. Not everybody wants that job. Often, we think troublesome issues and incidents in our life have little to do with our ability to write a mystery or a romance or a nature essay, but I believe that addressing our entire life with reverence, full awareness, and acceptance is our only hope if we want to both live and write honestly.

The Crossed Paths

One of the difficult parts about being a writer is that place where the solitary, creative writing path bumps up against the activities and expectations of the world. The crossed paths. Way before the cross was a religious symbol, it was a symbol of this meeting of the inner life and the outer life. *Webster's* says *cross* means "an affliction that tries one's virtue," which many of us would agree rather accurately describes writing some days.

This movement upward, as our growth meets culture and society, is like a seed sprouting and beginning to push up through the dark, moist earth, becoming more and more the particular plant it is destined to become, gaining strength and uniqueness. Then, suddenly, it breaks the surface of the earth. And weather, insects, and animals — in other words, life — begin to interact with its development. This is where the struggle occurs. This is the crux of our problem — *crux* being Latin for "cross."

For writers, this struggle means that creative energy pushes us up through a solitary, quiet, safe place of yearning and labor, allowing us to express ourselves, and then the urge to blossom meets everyday life. We might be okay for a while, as we keep our writing somewhat private, but in time, our sense of self is more that of a writer than that of some of the other identities we have taken on: mother, father, son, daughter, wife, husband, friend, employee, employer. We love our relationships as much as we always did; it's just that now we are writer-mother, writer-father, writer-friend. This urge to create colors everything. And it should. But just as a new sprout in a garden may be taken for a weed and not honored, we writers often feel that we live life in disguise, particularly if we haven't been widely published, because no one knows who we really are, often not even those we are partnered with, are parenting, or have befriended.

Lindy, for example, kept her writing so private the first several years that no one knew about it. When her daughters were young, they told friends that their mother wrote a lot of letters. As writers, we pretend to be among the normal people, all the while living in a way that no one, not even we ourselves, believes is normal at all. What we yearn for is to be acknowledged for who we *really* are. It may be the reason behind writing in the first place.

As writers, we choose a particular way of life. It is our business to see what others may miss; we see life as an exciting wilderness of connections, and we make it our work to discover these connections, mark the path through them, and pass the information on to others. We have noticed that we are after a larger experience of life than most. It doesn't make us better than others, but it does demand that we be more alert to life. And so it makes us different. We know that, and we like our differentness. Yet it is uncomfortable at times.

The discomfort may stem from the fact that our outer lives look and feel just like the lives of those that we view as asleep, a condition we are devoted to avoiding. When Kim works in his store, 150 people pass through each day and treat him as a service employee. They have no idea of who he feels he really is — a writer. "All day long, I explain things to amateur photographers, like: 'No, when the elk lose their antlers, they do not turn into moose,'" he says. "Nobody gives a darn that I've heard 'How are you?' dozens of times by noon. I've got to keep things fresh on my own."

Like Kim, most writers have day jobs that disguise their real selves. We pretend to be one of the others while really watching them carefully and writing down everything they say and do, like an undercover spy. Except, in our case, we don't want the disguise. We'd prefer to be known for the person we really are, not keep secret those ways of being in the world that stir our souls.

In certain respects, Kim has quit his day job. He says he is fully present when he's there, but not always in the way customers may expect when they walk in his door. "I entertain myself, ask questions, get to know people, do what I need to make it interesting as a writer." Kim sets out a pad with his writing project titled on the page. It may be an essay subject that he's gathering ideas for, or the need to fill in a character or story line. This written subject serves as a magnet throughout the day, drawing his material to him. At the end of the workday, the material serves as a list or guide that will direct his creative time, since, as many of us do, he needs help getting started.

Like Kim, I gather material while working at my shop, collecting physical descriptions, dialogue, or expressions from customers who pass through or pieces of information from the radio or newspapers. I call such things that come my way "day mail," in contrast to dreams, which are "night mail." Here are a few things that found me:

- A police officer visiting from Afton, Wyoming, said it is dull work; nothing happens after four o'clock. I asked, "Four in the morning?" He said, "No, afternoon. Everything comes to a standstill at four in the afternoon in Afton."

- Dora Mae works the switchboard located across the lobby from my shop at Snow King Resort. When she learned my first son weighed nine and a half pounds at birth, she said, "Why, honey, he was big enough to eat baled hay."

- A weather report in Jackson one January: "Due to the blizzard, travel outside the valley floor is not advisable today unless you are roped to several other people."

I loved telling that last one to my family in Ohio and Florida, though that didn't work in my favor when I invited them out for Christmas.

Deanna is a cashier at a large chain grocery store. She has worked there for years, is marvelously efficient, and is the fastest checker in the store. She begins talking with her customer while swiftly checking out a basketful of groceries, including the next customer in line, and often the one behind that, in an ongoing conversation that segues smoothly from topic to topic and customer to customer as they pass through her checkout station. At the end of the day, she often appears energized instead of drained. And she needs to be because after her store shift, Deanna works as a clown, creating toys out of balloons at restaurants, special events, and parties. Deanna is a wonderful role model for being our true self during our day job, because she doesn't turn into a grocery-pricing machine who won't look anybody in the eye but rather enlivens herself and everyone she meets during her workday.

Often, writers think the whole problem can be solved if only we can get published; then everyone will know who we really are. In other words, we can finally live as our real selves all the time, and not just when we're alone with our words. But this is frustrating because all the power for publishing appears to be in the hands of others. So we think living as our true selves is out there somewhere under the control of agents and editors.

It's not. The control for living our true selves lies within.

CHAPTER TWENTY-ONE

Writing Gifts

MUCH OF WHAT WE KNOW about being a writer is through the media. Writers are famous. They are Stephen King, who sells millions of books, makes millions of dollars, and gets run over by a van. So, if we want to be a writer, we aim for that — millions of books, millions of dollars, and hope to exclude being run over by a van.

I expected something on the order of that myself twenty-some years ago. But what happened instead were huge changes inwardly and wonderful openings outwardly — without the fame, money, or van parts.

Publishing, as many of you have discovered, doesn't really make all that much difference in our lives. I was in Texas, visiting Trevor and his family, when my first essay was published in a national magazine. I spotted the magazine at Barnes & Noble, bought it, and proudly dangled it in my son's face. He read it, said, "Nice," then, disregarding my new superior position in the world, continued to treat me as his mother.

We think, many of us, that we want publication. But my

experience suggests that what we may *really* yearn for are a few other things. One is *recognition* for who we really are. We are people who are creative, attentive, and deeply engaged with life. We're thinking and watching and making connections all the time. But we are doing this in solitude, and then, when we go out into the world to our jobs or the grocery store, nobody is acknowledging this vibrant self or the euphoria or the dark struggles we may have been experiencing while pursuing our creative work. Yet this inner activity fills us and makes us who we truly are in our private life or, sometimes, our secret life.

Also, we want *exchange* between our creative selves and others. We want our work to be received and responded to, along with being received and responded to as writers ourselves. The analogy I think of is preparing a huge, colorful feast of delicious foods. Long hours are spent planning, gathering ingredients, cooking. The table is set with the best dishes, fresh flowers, tall candles. Everything is ready for the guests...and nobody shows. Sure, we enjoyed the process, but we want to give this creative gift to someone and know it was received.

The third thing we want is *acceptance*, or inclusion in that world of like-minded people. We want community. We want to share our lives with other writers, discuss common interests, listen to other writers' experiences, and tell our own. We enjoy learning from those writers ahead of us on the path, and passing our teachings on to those behind us.

All three of these things — recognition, exchange, and acceptance — are lacking in the life of a private writer and are present in the life of a public writer. But we don't need publication, as we know it, to have our insides match our outsides — that particular honesty we crave in our lives. To publish means "to lay before the public," and that's what we're doing by attending writing workshops, conferences, and classes, participating in open-mike readings, and joining a writers' group: we are laying our creative selves before the public.

Over the years, a loosely organized group called the Teton Writers has met sporadically for lunch. One day, fifteen of us sat at a long table in a restaurant. The famed trial lawyer Gerry Spence shrugged out of his fringed leather jacket and started the conversation by saying, "We're all writers for one reason. We want to be published."

I sat directly across the table from Spence and jumped right on that statement. Since my work hadn't been published yet, it certainly wasn't seeing my words and name in print that drew me to my desk every day. It was the sheer aliveness of the flowing energy passing through me. I swear, I was getting smarter day by day, the way an infant's intelligence expands from loving stimulation. I hoped to rebut Spence's statement without disclosing that I had three unpublished novels stashed in my desk drawers, but being a trial lawyer, Spence probably needed that evidence.

So I confessed and said, "I am living proof that writing is not done in order to publish. I have been writing daily for fifteen years without publication. Writing is its own reward."

My story is that I won an argument with Gerry Spence, but other writers also came to my defense. Tim Sandlin, author of *Lydia* and several other novels, said he wouldn't stop writing even if he had to pay someone else to let him do it. And in fact, it had come down to that for him when he had borrowed money at a high interest rate in between dishwashing jobs just to keep going, before his novels and screenplays supported him. Warren Adler, author of *War of the Roses*, added that he felt like a lucky man to sit at his desk and create imaginary worlds of his own every day. Warren said that writing, for him, was a calling, like the priesthood.

After those years of outer inactivity in my writing life, a sudden abundance of "laying before the public" occurred. During six weeks one spring, my essays were published in three national magazines and two anthologies, I won first place in a national fiction competition, and I was invited to conduct three workshops. But what really affected my life as a public writer was a local open-mike reading in which I participated. And even better than that was the morning after, when I walked into Pearl Street Bagels to pick up my mocha latte on the way to my shop and greeted two other people who knew from that reading that I was a writer. This acknowledgment of my true self during the course of my daily routine produced the most affirmation and satisfaction. The event has been repeated but, even these many years later, never topped, despite having the Penguin Group publish my novels. This is an experience we can all enjoy in our own communities.

The writer Ron Carlson once said to me when I was bemoaning the dearth of recognition as a writer, "You are gathering the inventory; something is bound to happen eventually. Keep writing." He was right, and this is true for a kind of inner inventory we are gathering as well. Self-knowledge takes time and a storehouse of experiences. The advice is the same: *keep writing*.

The Partnering of Essence and Ego

This desire to be known to ourselves and others as a writer has two parts. One is pure ego; the other is pure essence — inner spirit.

Our inner essence doesn't care about judgments that concern the ego, such as: Shouldn't we have accomplished more by our age (whatever that age may be)? Shouldn't we have more money to show for our work, more recognition? Ego is nothing but an insatiable pest; feed it one publication or prize, and it wants another. The inner being, however, the source of our creative force, doesn't distinguish success from failure, doesn't count money, doesn't keep track of time. Our inner self just wants to work and play; it wants to create.

If we address our attention and energy to our inner essence, it will in time turn ego into a useful entity for our inner selves. Ego can help us in much the same way as an aide-de-camp, who is an assistant to a superior. For example, my ego got me dressed decently this morning, and it will protect me from serious damage to my spirit that could arise from critical barbs as I do my work. And it will defend my personal boundaries for me when the telephone rings or a neighbor asks for a favor. My ego, if it knows its place, will work as an assistant to the executive commander, which is my inner essence.

Without the inner essence, ego collapses, like an eggshell without an egg inside. Pretty fragile. Unless the ego petrifies — which explains some public figures to me.

The best care and feeding of a writer is to address the inner essence. Once we pull our attention from out there, where others have control, to in here, where we have total reign, we really begin to live as writers. Our egos want the outer acknowledgment; our inner selves want the fulfillment of living each moment as a writer. Once we succeed there, the rest of it no longer matters.

The Gifts We Give

If we feel that our yearning to live creative lives sets us apart from others, it's true; it does. When Joseph Campbell talks about the Arthurian legend and the search for the Grail as a metaphor for the search for life's meaning, he tells us that each of the knights stepped into the forest at the darkest part. Creative people are drawn to the darkest part of the forest, the place where the questions are hanging thick from the trees and the answers are nowhere to be found. We are lured into the forest by the questions. And we enter the forest, grab hold of those questions, and give them language, labels, contexts, connections. This is our gift to the world as writers. We acknowledge the life around us, sometimes make sense of it, often soothe one another, always bear witness. These are important gifts.

Wayne Muller, an author and the founder of an organization called Bread for the Journey, says, "The world aches for your gift. Whatever it is, the world aches for your gift."

If writing gives you a sense of expansiveness, satisfaction, joy, completion, stimulation, spiritedness, then this is what you are adding to the world every time you do your work. That is no small thing.

Living consciously is a soul choice, a way of being in the world, a chosen filter for our experiences. And beyond what it means to us is what it means to others to have us in the world. We take in and give back out. We watch and listen to the stories within us and around us, and we reflect them back to others. Our stories enhance lives, heal souls, teach, and soothe. I came across this happy ending to a Native American tale: "Plenty of food, shelter and stories to keep them." These are people who had all they needed for a good life.

Epictetus, a Greek philosopher from the first century, said, "You are a distinct portion of the essence of God; and contain part of [God] in yourself." About here, I imagine his voice rising in irritation. "Do you not know that it is the Divine you feed, the Divine you exercise?" Now he's about to actually yell. "You carry a God about with you, poor wretch, and know nothing of it!"

We've been suspecting this. That we "poor wretches" carry something of the divine within us. Yet when I read the newsletter from the Wyoming Arts Council and spot the heading, "Grant Money for the Underserved," I read it as saying, "Grant Money for the Undeserved." I perk up and think, "Hmm, this might be something for me."

It makes me laugh to catch myself, but I wonder, too, why I think I am not deserving of money set aside for the arts. I suspect I am not alone among writers and artists, because we do not tend to honor our work unless it is honored by others. So that even receiving a grant for the "undeserved" strikes me as an opening to recognition, exchange, and acceptance, those three things my inner essence wants and my ego goes looking for.

A Sacred Art

If we think that what we write doesn't deserve to be honored, then consider the importance of the simple, fun books we read as a child — how they began our life as a reader, then a writer. We may have been hooked on comic books. Craved them. And then craved other books; and then craved time alone, with or without a book; then craved writing down what we were learning about life, first in journals for ourselves and then into books for others.

Wallace Black Elk, author of *Black Elk: The Sacred Ways of a Lakota*, once lived the life of a *heyoka*, a clown who amuses the tribe by saying and doing the exact opposite of the norm — for example, going naked outside in the winter, washing in dirt, riding a horse facing the tail. Black Elk served as a *heyoka* for one year in preparation for becoming a medicine man. He believed his work as a clown was good training for guiding his tribe's spirits, because clowning suspended tradition, lifted the people out of their rutted thinking, and offered fresh perspective and relief from the sobering reality of life. All skills necessary for shamans.

As writers, we play the same role in our society that a *heyoka* or shaman does in native societies. We reflect thought and action back to the people in our community in a nonaggressive, sometimes humorous way. We bring into consciousness and put into words what otherwise might remain in the unspoken unconsciousness of ourselves and our community. Just as it is the job of shamans in native cultures to announce the larger patterns — the weather, the movement of the herds that feed the tribe — we are the ones assigned to be most awake. This is our contribution. We notice and alert the people to ideas, feelings, movements, and changes that are in the transpersonal consciousness. It is as if we are the speakers for Jung's collective unconscious or Rupert Sheldrake's morphic field.

As the medicine men and wise women of our culture, it is our job:

To be first aware

To make connections

To detect patterns

To notify others

To bring into consciousness and put into words what otherwise would remain in the unconscious of ourselves and our community

To remember that the world needs our gifts

Why We Write

We write for the same reasons we read. We write so we can read about ourselves. And read so we can write about ourselves. We write/read for pleasure, to seek knowledge, to expand our perspectives, to help us discover or further ourselves along our path. We write/read to connect our awareness with what we've always known, to educate ourselves — or re-remember. We write/read to learn about other people, places, and times, to deepen and broaden ourselves.

In short, we write for two main reasons: We write for self-knowledge. We write for engagement with other interesting minds.

Try This

Take a single memory, reaching far, far back, either to early childhood or to early in a relationship that troubles you. Just as if you were doodling or doing a quick sketch, write it down. No need for full sentences; use phrases, a list. Write it down however it occurs to you. Include details and emotions. If you get stuck, write about the feeling the memory stirs in you now.

Do this exercise at odd moments in your day: leaning against the kitchen counter waiting for your coffee to brew, stalled in traffic, on hold during phone calls. Don't make a big deal out of it; just sketch.

Jill gained self-knowledge in sketching out a single memory. She wrote: "I was five, maybe only four. I wore a blue dotted Swiss pinafore, the house was damp and chilly, my mother was hurried. 'Get that hair off your face, you look like a rag picker.' She pulled it tightly off my forehead and pinned it with a barrette on top of my head. I didn't look like myself and felt awkward in my body all day."

This sketch may seem unimportant at first glance, but it revealed a lot to Jill about herself, once she gave it her attention. Moments after writing this brief snatch of memory, Jill recalled how her mother would often carefully dress her in her best clothes and then insult her. "You look like a ragamuffin." "I'm embarrassed to be seen with you." So even now as an adult, Jill feels self-conscious dressing up for special occasions. She slips on a lovely long velvet dress with a scooped neck and the gold necklace her husband gave her, then at the last minute pulls on a pair of purple leather cowboy boots with orange and yellow butterflies stitched on them. There. She's out of the running for trying to look conventionally well dressed. Her mother would have been speechless.

Along with this new view of Jill's dress-up complex came the insight that her mother wasn't insulting Jill at all, but rather herself. Jill's spunky twenty-three-year-old mother juggled money needed for heating fuel with the desire to dress her family well. It was her mother's fear and misgivings that Jill felt the brunt of. A rush of love for her mother soaked into Jill at this memory, and she recalled that many times in her life, her mother also told Jill that she was beautiful. Jill determined that the next time she got five minutes, she'd sketch one of those memories.

This is how we know ourselves and track our lives. Such jottings are a verbal photographic album. After every one of these sketches, we are aligned more and more to our bodies and to that dark shadow of the unknown that follows us around. Bit by bit, we cast light upon the hidden and claim it: this, too, is part of me.

Try This

Engage with other interesting minds by responding to quotations. In writing, interact with any of the following statements with which you feel an affinity or to which you have a response.

Let the beauty we love be what we do.
— Rumi

If you don't get what you want, it is a sign you did not seriously want it, or that you tried to bargain over the price.
— Rudyard Kipling

It's the soul's duty to be loyal to its own desires.
— Rebecca West

You are in that place to testify.
— Emerson

The highest way asks nothing hard.
— Seng-ts'an

And then let the man think of the Spirit as streaming, pouring,
rushing and shining into him from all sides while he stands quiet.
— Plotinus

By all means, use sometimes to be alone,
Salute thyself: see what thy soul doth wear....
And tumble up and down what thou findst there.
— George Herbert

Attention — yes!
— Dalai Lama

Expect nothing; live frugally on surprise.
— Alice Walker

You can't see the gift in what you resist.
— Penney Peirce

If you bring forth what is within you,
what is within you will save you.
— Jesus, Gospel of Thomas

I want to write but more than that, I want to bring out
all kinds of things that lie buried deep in my heart.
— Anne Frank

Really it just delights me to write.
— Eudora Welty

The Earthweave

LIVING BESIDE TWO OF OUR COUNTRY'S NATIONAL PARKS, Grand Teton National Park and Yellowstone, the people of Jackson Hole, Wyoming, acknowledge a responsibility for protecting wilderness. We engage in forums that discuss this responsibility and explore the value of wilderness to humans. Tens of thousands travel here from all over the world to experience the wildlands and the animals that live in them. I joke that we are a valley of nurses, tending these weary visitors that arrive for their vacations winter and summer. Many step off the planes flat eyed, armored, heavy-footed, though some are immediately shocked into wakefulness by the abrupt rise of mountain spires, the spread of open spaces, the easy smiles of the locals, and the calm gaze of elk and moose feeding beside the road to town. Some need several days before they begin noticing their surroundings. Yet, eventually, the wildness outside leads to the wildness within, that place that gives space and reflects truth and accepts everything.

Wilderness gives us room — silence and space and time

— to be without judgment, to acknowledge our shadows, to hear and ponder and rove our memories and dreams. Perspective follows. Free-range thinking and feeling lead to wisdom and calm, and a comfort with the unanswered, with mystery. With wildness.

In the wilderness, the is-ness is reflected back to us with the clarity of pure water. If we value truth and clarity within, we will demand purity in our air and water without. If we value creative energy within, we will value creative energy without, as it is expressed in the forests, oceans, swamps, mountains, and deserts. And we will protect them.

When we still the mind, we inhabit the true essence of being — not doing, achieving, conjuring. Being. In this stillness, this state of being-ness, we are in wilderness. No road signs, no paved pathways, no itinerary. If we are uneasy in the wilderness of our own being-ness or, as is common, do not venture there at all, will we value the wilderness of the natural world? Don't the two reflect each other? And doesn't the way we address our own inner wilderness reflect the way we treat the small pockets of wilderness remaining on earth? Our inner work, the acknowledgment and expression of our own creative energy, stretches all the way to the remote reaches of the planet.

There was a time when we lived as one with nature unselfconsciously, as a babe at the breast of its mother. To regain this intimacy with nature in a conscious manner, we bring our unconscious love to awareness by naming, describing, and interacting. In time, our relationship will no longer separate into yin and yang, subject and object, self and observer. As happens in meditation, prayer, and falling in love, the distinction between us and other diffuses, and we again become one. All the great religions and philosophies of the world hold this state of oneness as the highest experience.

We must discuss the natural world as separate from ourselves in order to take it apart, name its pieces, and describe its parts, until our knowledge becomes an intimate interaction between ourselves and the natural world through the unearthing of our stories.

Self and nature are not two separate entities, but one being. To reclaim that condition, we go not backward to unconsciousness but rather forward through separation to conscious merging into oneness, spiraling skyward in cycles of growth, the way the trunk of the Engelmann spruce beside my cabin porch spirals in its growth upward from darkness to sunlight and around again, reaching skyward.

This summer, my friend Bette and I drove eighty-five miles over a snowy mountain pass to do a day hike to Lake Louise. We arrived at the trailhead, hoisted our backpacks, and began our climb. Soon, we began to follow cairns that marked the path when it disappeared into rock slabs that hung over the steep slopes. In a few hours, we reached Lake Louise, and both of us gasped at the beauty of the deep teal-blue water, the mountains ringing the small lake, the barn-sized boulders emerging from it. Bette read the guidebook and said, "The Native Americans called one of these ranges the Shining Mountains." She pointed to a line of snowy peaks glinting in the far distance and said, "Maybe those." They were shining alright. Some of those snowfields were glaciers thousands of years old. Directly beside us rose sheer rock slopes all the way to the puffy clouds that billowed like circus tents above us. The sun was hidden in one of those clouds. As I looked at the rock-faced slope, the sun abruptly popped out, and the entire rock mountain sparked into a glistening shimmer of light. Once again, I gasped at the beauty.

When my eyes adjusted to the brilliance, I could see that the sun reflected off myriad streams of water seeping, then fanning, across the face of the mountain.

"Bette, look."

Bette said, "Maybe *these* are the Shining Mountains."

Earlier that morning, before we began our hike, the dirt road to the trailhead took us past petroglyphs hundreds of years old. We stopped the car, got out, and climbed up hillsides to see the drawings closer and to wonder about the people who had etched the figures of bighorns into the rock. At the moment that I caught the sun reflecting off the water transuding the face of the mountain, I felt a further connection with those same people, who had also surely experienced this sight so long ago. For the luminous effect to occur, the timing must be right, with the sun angled in a blue sky just opposite the rock face. The Native Americans who carved the petroglyphs and lived here enjoyed this sight often. For my friend and me, the gift of this sight was synchronistic, and I will never forget how the moment was enhanced by the link of light and earth and my presence there beside the shining mountain.

The experience reminded me of seeing the spiderweb woven around the pine tree on Snow King Mountain while doing a Spirit Walk. One moment, I do not see it; the next moment, light catches the web and reflects back to me a beauty that clutches my heart. Writing this book has been a similar experience for me. One moment, I see the web of light. I understand the profound connection between all living things. I know I want to share the awareness and live within it. The next moment, it disappears, and I question whether anything was there at all. Yet each experience of opening myself to the creative energy of nature beckons another response from the natural world that, like answered prayers, sends the roots of my being deeper into the earth and invites my spirit to soar higher.

The one thing I wish for each of us in this world is the willingness to experience the weave of energy that binds all living things and pulsates within each of us, breathing in, breathing out. Trees laced in light and the shine of water-veined mountains are reminders of the earthweave.

Keep watching.

Keep writing.

Acknowledgments

I WROTE THIS BOOK because I needed to learn everything in it and wanted to remember everything I'd learned. The authors quoted in the book and listed in the back, plus many more teachers along the way, contributed to my waking, incomplete as it is, and I'm grateful to them.

My agent, Meredith Kaffel, is the angel who opened the door to the outside world. She gave her energy and expertise to my manuscript wholeheartedly. I'm grateful for her warm spirit and insightful mind. My editor, Jason Gardner at New World Library, took a chance with this book, and I am so pleased that he did. Both Jason and my copyeditor, Mark Colucci, are caring and perceptive readers who have used their wisdom to make this a better book. I thank all the bright people at New World Library who have worked on behalf of *Writing Wild*.

For further literary support, I thank writers Patti Sherlock, Susan Marsh, and Elaine Mansfield, who read and critiqued and cheered me on. And for help in the very early stages of writing, I thank Kristen Corbett, Geneen Haugen, and Connie Wieneke.

All along, I have been supported by Tim Sandlin and the Jackson Hole Writers Conference, Artists and Writers, the Wyoming Arts Council, and Hedgebrook.

I thank the friends and family members mentioned in the book for their contributions. Special thanks to my husband, John Buhler, for his love and support.

Recommended Reading

Campbell, Joseph. *The Power of Myth*. With Bill Moyers. New York: Doubleday, 1988. See also Campbell's other books, talks, and interviews.

Csikszentmihalyi, Mihaly. *Creativity: Flow and the Psychology of Discovery and Invention*. New York: HarperCollins, 1996.

————. *Flow: The Psychology of Optimal Experience*. New York: Harper & Row, 1990.

Goldberg, Natalie. *Writing Down the Bones: Freeing the Writer Within*. Boston: Shambhala, 1986.

Hinchman, Hannah. *A Trail through Leaves: The Journal as a Path to Place*. New York: Norton, 1997.

Jung, C. G. *Memories, Dreams, Reflections*. Edited by Aniela Jaffé. Translated by Richard Winston and Clara Winston. New York: Vintage Books, 1989. See also Jung's other works.

MacEowen, Frank. *The Mist-Filled Path: Celtic Wisdom for Exiles, Wanderers, and Seekers*. Novato, CA: New World Library, 2002.

Metzner, Ralph. *Green Psychology: Transforming Our Relationship to the Earth*. Rochester, VT: Park Street Press, 1999.

————. *The Unfolding Self: Varieties of Transformative Experience*. Novato, CA: Origin Press, 1986.

Mindell, Arnold. *Working on Yourself Alone: Inner Dreambody Work*. London: Arkana, 1990.

Northrup, Christiane. *Women's Bodies, Women's Wisdom: Creating Physical and Emotional Health and Healing*. New York: Bantam Books, 1994.

Palmer, Wendy. *The Intuitive Body: Aikido as a Clairsentient Practice*. Berkeley, CA: North Atlantic Books, 1994.

Peirce, Penney. *The Intuitive Way: A Guide to Living from Inner Wisdom*. Hillsboro, OR: Beyond Words, 1997.

Pennebaker, James W. *Opening Up: The Healing Power of Expressing Emotions*. New York: Guilford Press, 1990.

Rogers, Pattiann. *The Dream of the Marsh Wren: Writing as Reciprocal Creation*. Minneapolis: Milkweed Editions, 1999.

Stafford, William. *Crossing Unmarked Snow: Further Views on the Writer's Vocation*. Edited by Paul Merchant and Vincent Wixon. Ann Arbor: University of Michigan Press, 1998.

Three Initiates. *The Kybalion: A Study of the Hermetic Philosophy of Ancient Egypt and Greece*. Mokelumne Hill, CA: Health Research, 1970. Several print editions of *The Kybalion* are available; an online version is available at www.gutenberg.org/ebooks/14209.

Wilkinson, Tanya. *Medea's Folly: Women, Relationships, and the Search for Intimacy*. Berkeley, CA: PageMill Press, 1998.

Woodman, Marion. *Bone: Dying into Life*. New York: Penguin Compass, 2000. See also Woodman's other books, talks, and interviews.

About the Author

TINA WELLING is the author of the novels *Cowboys Never Cry*, *Fairy Tale Blues*, and *Crybaby Ranch*, all published by NAL Accent / Penguin. She has been a member of the Jackson Hole Writers Conference faculty for fifteen years, and has been conducting her Writing Wild workshops for ten years. She also leads and facilitates the Writers in the Park workshop at Grand Teton National Park. Her nonfiction has appeared in *Body & Soul*, *Shambhala Sun*, *Natural Health*, *The Writer*, and four anthologies. She is a longtime resident of Jackson Hole, Wyoming, where she owned a retail business at the ski resort for twenty-five years. She is an active hiker and cross country skier. Her website is www.tinawelling.com.